ONE FAMILY'S JOURNEY THROUGH

ALZHEIMER'S

MARY B. WALSH

Tyndale House Publishers, Inc.
Wheaton, Illinois

Visit Tyndale's exciting Web site at www.tyndale.com

Designed by Julie Chen

Edited by James Kraus

Library of Congress Cataloging-in-Publication Data

Walsh, Mary B.
   One family's journey through Alzheimer's / Mary B. Walsh.
     p. cm.
   ISBN 0-8423-4095-5 (sc)
     1. Alzheimer's disease—Patients—Biography.   2. Walsh family.   3. Alzheimer's
disease—Religious aspects—Christianity.   4. Walsh, Mary B.   I. Title.

RC523.2.W355 2000
362.1′96831′0092—dc21
[B]   00-059921

Printed in the United States of America

04   03   02   01   00
6   5   4   3   2   1

$\mathcal{T}$HANK $\mathcal{Y}$OU!

$\mathcal{S}$pecial thanks to my best friend and husband, Eddie, for his tireless efforts and endless patience with my limited technical knowledge—and to think we are still best friends!

Thanks to my mom for her constant support and wonderful example of facing life's difficulties with patience and even a sense of humor.

And thanks to my four wonderful children—Jamie, Chris, Dawn, and David—for giving of themselves in so many ways these past years.

I would like to thank my friend Kelley Dold for sacrificing her valuable housecleaning time to give me her last-minute input—or better said—for sacrificing her housecleaning time to give me her valuable input. Thanks, Kelley. (I know how you hated to give it up.)

Last of all, but certainly not least, to our dear Aunt Flip—you're a trooper!

TABLE OF CONTENTS

$\mathcal{H}$ad anyone told me that I would be dedicating this book to the memory of my father, Wallace M. Kunkel, I would have said, "Oh, no not that!" I didn't think I could face that loss. Yet, only months before the completion of the final chapter, that loss came into my life.

Rarely has a daughter had the pleasure of sharing her life with a dad who so thoroughly loved her. I miss him profoundly.

My dad had many and varied talents, but I dedicate this book to my dad, the writer.

As a little girl, I recall many evenings running into the dining room of our home to find him sitting at his typewriter, deep in thought. I would climb up onto his knee and watch his fingers move smoothly over the keyboard, his mind off in another place, another time. He'd come back for a moment as if surprised to see me. He'd hug me and kiss me goodnight.

"Goodnight, Mame-doll!" he'd say. I'd skip off to bed and fall asleep to the rhythmic sound of his typewriter as he worked well into the night.

That old typewriter was soon replaced with a fancy electric machine. The lullaby wasn't the same, but the faint tapping could still be heard as I dropped off to sleep. By the time that machine was outdated and my husband surprised him with a spanking new computer, I was busy raising children; yet I would fall asleep at night well aware that my dad was up typing into the wee hours of the morning, totally engrossed in another era—perhaps one that was not quite so complex. I would awaken some mornings to an E-mail note from him, sent at an hour most of us are sleeping soundly.

Many days I would stop by to see him, and my young children would climb up onto their grandpa's lap and watch his fingers move swiftly over the keyboard (now by memory, as most of his sight was lost to diabetes). Always delighted by the intrusion, he would stop to hug them and maybe share some exciting genealogical discovery he had made. They'd hop down and run off, and he would go back to work.

Inspired by his passion for writing, I wrote poems and stories throughout my childhood. Once in a while, if I thought it was pretty decent, I'd run downstairs and have my dad read it. If he said, "That's pretty cute, Mame!" I'd run back up and start over. I knew that "pretty cute" wasn't very good.

As I got older, a few poems merited a "That's real fine, Mame!" and I knew I was progressing. It was important to me because I respected my dad, the writer.

As he lay in his hospital bed only weeks before he died, he was editing chapters of this book. I received a surprising call one evening. It was my dad, and although he was sick and in terrible pain he'd called to tell me he had finished editing chapter 2.

"Mame, this is absolutely spectacular!"

I cried as I heard his words—for many reasons. Of course I was thrilled by his approval, but I also knew how hard it was for him to read it at all. I was concerned that he would not live to read the remaining chapters.

He did not, but I promised him I would finish it.

And so I have.

This is for you, Dad!

*T*here are those experiences in our lives that are so difficult, yet afterwards we realize it was the only way. Childbirth is one of those experiences. Taking part in this divine drama, we share in a bit of life so profound that words simply fall short.

Following the exhausting delivery of our firstborn child, I turned to my mother and husband's grandmother and asked why they had never told me what I was in for. I'll never forget the expressions on their faces. Without a word they conveyed to me somewhat of a secret among mothers.

"How could we tell you?" their expressions said.

"And now you know."

There are those experiences in our lives that are so difficult, yet afterwards we realize that it was the only way. We've experienced a bit of life so profound that words simply fall short.

I would not have sent that baby back for anything.

Caring for an elderly loved one stricken with Alzheimer's disease has proven to be just such an experience.

✠   ✠   ✠

I wrote this opening statement several years ago for an article published in an elder care newsletter. Little did I realize then the depth of the analogy—how very similar to that first labor and delivery the care of an Alzheimer's victim would prove to be.

At that time, we had been caring for Gram in our home for the nearly four years since her diagnosis with Alzheimer's. I shared some of the painful and trying experiences we had been through as a family and the heartbreak of her rapid decline. In the back of my mind I believed the worst to be over. I still had the stamina and the attitude that, by God's grace, we would handle the situation.

I now see that those struggles were just the beginning, the "birth pangs" of the laborious experience that lay ahead of us. In that labor room, during those seemingly endless hours of heavy labor, I reached a crucial moment when I felt as though I could not go on. I really wanted to give up! That feeling also lay ahead for us in the care of Gram.

There eventually came a time of transition when her condition suddenly changed. There was no more fight, no more struggle to hold on to all she held dear. Although she was now unable to care for her most basic needs and required around-the-clock attention, I once again believed we'd see the situation through.

As a Christian—and believing Gram to have also trusted Christ for her salvation—I saw her death as her deliverance. Although she experienced very little physical pain throughout her illness, the mental torment was incredible.

We all miss her but are thankful that her fight is over. She is whole once again—no, better than whole—in his glorious presence.

I said concerning the delivery of my firstborn, "I would not have sent that baby back for anything." Looking back on this experience I have come to the very same conclusion. As difficult as it turned out to be, I know it was the only way. I shared in the toughest days of her life, realizing she would have done the same for me.

This book began as entries in a journal that I have kept since early in my marriage, twenty years ago. As the years passed, this story unfolded—so different a story than what my family and I had planned or hoped for. Writing became a necessary outlet for the struggles I faced. And I enjoyed it. The more I wrote, the clearer it became that my story is only one of thousands that could be shared. Families all over the world care for loved ones and are in similar, equally hard situations—wishing that others could understand. They may never have the opportunity to write about it—so my story is also their story.

I hope that I might encourage others to go on—to not give up—by sharing our struggles, our many failures, yet our ultimate survival as a family.

1

"*I*ncredible! Take a look at those maple trees," my husband exclaimed. The leaves were at their perfect autumn peak. Each turn down the mountain road brought to mind such pleasant memories: the neatly kept stone houses that edged the road—each with its own character, ripened by age—the quaint little general store.

Schooley's Mountain Road in northern New Jersey wasn't just any mountain road. We had spent seven wonderful years living in an old farmhouse nestled in the middle of a six hundred-acre horse farm just off that road.

We were back in the area for a visit. As we neared a familiar hairpin curve, I could see the gravel driveway to our former home.

Our three oldest children had been born before our move to Schooley's Mountain Road. Jamie and Chris were two years apart. Then, as if to ease the anxiety of redheaded Christopher's approach toward the "terrible twos," we were blessed with a dainty little girl. Born at the first whisper of daylight on a day approaching Christmas, we named her, appropriately, Dawn Angel.

Her dark pink skin tone and soft, shiny black hair defied expectation. She brought to mind images of a revered, lone Cherokee great-great-grandmother of whom my dad often spoke. Her delicate pink sweaters and ruffled petticoats were a pleasant addition to the ever-mounting laundry basket in the Walsh home.

The year we moved into the farmhouse, Dawn was two years old. I was then informed by my doctor that yet another baby was on the way. To my astonishment and Ed's utter delight, an ultra-sound revealed an added surprise. There was not one baby on the way, but two. We were going to have twins!

"Remember the first months in that house, Eddie?" I asked, straining to get a peek at it, set back off the road. How could we ever forget?

On the morning of the big move to that farmhouse on Schooley's Mountain Road, I was alarmed by some disturbing pregnancy signs and rushed to my obstetrician. He ordered me off my feet—possibly for the remainder of the pregnancy. My part in the attempt to save my babies was to "do nothing."

"I want you to make the Queen of Sheba look like a worka-holic," he instructed me.

"Off my feet," I mused as I surrendered to the couch, watch-ing my three little roughneck children play hide-and-seek amidst the boxes piled high.

Eddie and I had a way of moving into houses that needed "reconstructing." I had always found it a real challenge to take an apartment or house in dire need and transform it into a cozy, livable home. Of our many opportunities, I viewed the farmhouse as the ultimate challenge. I, however, was starting out at a definite disadvantage—in a horizontal position.

I surveyed the living room, which ran the full width of the front of the house. It had such possibilities! There was a charming little stone fireplace tucked into the corner of the room by the staircase. At the landing were built-in bookshelves and a cupboard for firewood. Large double windows graced the sides of the front door. There were also single windows at each side of the room. I pictured myself pulling out my sewing machine and spending a few evenings making curtains from yards of unbleached muslin. I was not intimidated by the many windows, but from my prone posi-tion they appeared immense and ominous.

Before I could convince myself just how bleak my situation was, help arrived. Friends and family unpacked, painted, and prepared what turned out to be months of meals, making it possible for me to do what I thought was impossible—stay off my feet. As the months passed, we were hopeful that our babies would survive.

"If you go into labor at twenty-five weeks, go straight to St. Joseph's Children's Hospital. They have all the facilities necessary to keep the twins alive," my doctor assured me.

On New Year's day, at twenty-six weeks, I was wakened by contractions—the real thing. Hoping they would settle down, I stayed in bed. I could see the darkening winter sky through my window and hear the sound of Ed's chain saw. He had been gathering firewood in the backyard all morning with the children's help. Normally these were pleasant sounds—the preparation for a coming storm—our children's footsteps on the back stairs, dropping wood onto the porch.

I tried to sleep, but each time I dozed off I was jolted back to reality. I was facing the very real possibility that one or both of my babies might not make it. Ed walked into the room and we looked at one another. We both knew it was time. I dressed, shivering from both the cold and the fear of the unknown ahead.

"Let's pray," Ed said. Seated together on the edge of the bed, we bowed our heads and prayed. The shivering stopped as I realized the outcome had always been in the Lord's hands. I had peace. We left for the hospital.

Following seven hours of labor, the first baby was stillborn. It was a boy. The second baby, also a boy, was born within the hour and died immediately. I was overwhelmed at how much they resembled our oldest son, Jamie, and how perfectly developed they were—complete with full heads of beautiful, jet-black hair. The sight of them drew deep within my heart a longing for that time when all tears will be wiped away and when there will be no more dying. During that very sad time I was comforted by what has now become one of my favorite Psalms:

MY FRAME WAS NOT HIDDEN FROM YOU WHEN I WAS MADE IN THE SECRET PLACE. WHEN I WAS WOVEN TOGETHER IN THE DEPTHS OF THE EARTH, YOUR EYES SAW MY UNFORMED BODY. ALL THE DAYS

I did not need to torment myself with What if? and Couldn't they have done more? All their days had been ordained for them.

I have never taken this comfort for granted.

How often the Lord has used the Psalms of David to bring me comfort and peace. That may have had a lot to do with my desire to name our next child "David"—born two years after the twins died. He brought such joy and healing to our family.

My memories of those years are "wonderful." We pulled together, prayed together, struggled together. It was wonderful.

✠   ✠   ✠

"Let's drive by Gram's house," I suggested as we continued down the road toward the town.

We often made this trip down the mountain road to Grandma Walsh's house. Many such visits on spectacular autumn days stand out in my mind. We would drive down her long paved driveway, admiring the two acres that she and her sister Margaretta kept neatly mowed and trimmed. How we loved seeing the beautiful towering pines and flowering trees that Gram and her husband had planted through the years.

Her garden announced the seasons with bursts of color. Spring brought tulips and daffodils. Poppies grew huge in her garden. They bowed down to make room for mums.

When we arrived, the doors of our station wagon would fly open almost simultaneously with the screen door of her house. Our little ones would scurry up the walk to greet their great-grandma strutting toward them, clapping her hands together in sheer pleasure, grinning from ear to ear. She did indeed strut. Her posture, so elegantly erect, told the world that life was beautiful and that she was in control. I could not imagine her any other way.

✠   ✠   ✠

Her confidence did not come from an easy life. Her childhood, a time she rarely discussed, was one of great turmoil. When her

oldest son's marriage fell apart, she and her husband took the
responsibility of raising his three young children. Ed, my
husband, was the oldest child. Grandpa Walsh died unexpectedly
of a heart attack at the age of fifty, and Gram was devastated. The
shock and grief threatened to undo her. But she realized the
tremendous task she was left with and went to work.

In a desperate attempt to keep busy and escape the emptiness
of her loss, she held down two jobs, catching a little sleep in
between. She worked a full day in the ladies' department of a well-
known clothing store, returned for dinner and a cup of tea, then
worked the late shift in a local nursing home.

"I pray to God I will never need to be taken care of when I'm
old!" she would shudder upon returning home late at night. "I
hope to die before my faculties fail me," she would add as if she
would have it no other way.

Her sister Margaretta faithfully took care of the house. They
made quite a team. Margaretta had never married and had always
lived with Gram and her husband. She was a welcome and pleasant
addition to their home, always putting the needs of others before
her own. She worked at a nearby government arsenal, and all the
rest of her time was taken up caring for the three children. Her
name, however, was a real problem for the children—they all had
trouble pronouncing "Aunt Margaretta." So they dubbed her
"Flip" with great affection. It suited her, and Flip has been her
name ever since.

Gram was most definitely the dominant of the two sisters,
having the final word in discussions and decisions. Flip always
complied, doing much as she was told. It was not, however, done
grudgingly. One could sense the deep love and admiration she had
for her older sister.

Raising three teenagers in the 1960s presented yet new chal-
lenges to Gram's "never say die" attitude. Although Ed was somewhat of a taxing youth, involving himself in the dangerous drug
culture of the times, Gram never gave up loving him or hoping
that he would soon settle down. Following his graduation from
high school in 1970, he began working in a small company owned

by my dad, Wallace Kunkle. Ed was his right-hand man, and I was the boss's daughter—definitely love at first sight. There are some who say that it doesn't happen that way—but it did.

I believe Gram hoped that Ed's and my relationship would be enough to bring him around. There came a point, however, when my love was not enough to keep us together.

Totally beguiled by the independent mindset of the 1960s, having questioned and disregarded all "traditional" values, we were left with such emptiness. Our relationship survived two years—but I reached a point where I could not take any more.

Late one night Ed picked up a book his sister had brought home from school entitled *The Jesus Generation* by Billy Graham. He read of the forgiveness for sin that is available to anyone who will turn to Christ. New life was the promise.

"It's all going to be different now, Mary," he assured me. "I can't tell you exactly what has happened, but it has to do with the Bible and Jesus Christ."

I had heard his empty promises before, but I was startled by something new in his eyes. Formerly dulled by drugs and alcohol, they were now clean and sparkling. I realized that I was looking at a new man—the new creation spoken of in the Bible.

THEREFORE, IF ANYONE IS IN CHRIST, HE IS A NEW CREATION; THE OLD HAS GONE, THE NEW HAS COME!   2 CORINTHIANS 5:17, NIV

Within a short time, the Lord graciously brought me to himself also. My life had been filled with hopelessness and futility and was now filled with tremendous joy and peace.

Our excitement could not be contained. We spent the following months visiting our friends and telling them of our new life in Christ. It was obvious that there had indeed been a drastic change. To some it was unbelievable. To others I'm sure we were quite obnoxious.

We were soon tagged "The God Squad."

And within six months we were married.

✠   ✠   ✠

Then, seemingly overnight, we found ourselves with a car full of children scrambling to get out and greet their great-grandmother as she strode with open arms to meet them.

Her open door on fall days like this would let out faint whispers of nutmeg—apple pie for sure. The children would run inside ahead of us.

Gram's great-grandchildren were her delight. "Mother," she would often call me, "come in and see what I have up on needles for the young man!" She would then display a sweater or knitted snowsuit boasting some intricate pattern. A day without something "up on needles" was rare, for it was no sooner on the needles than it was off the needles. She worked fast and furious. If she spotted the slightest flaw, it came out—no matter how long she had worked. Gram's work had to be perfect.

"It's Friday. Why don't I pick the children up later and you two go out and have a ball?"

She seemed to relive her love for her husband through our love for each other. If she walked in on us hugging or kissing, she would glow with an air of sweet reminiscence.

"That's a beautiful sight!" she would say. She would speak fondly of her husband and point to the delicate silver wedding band she wore.

"This ring has never been off my finger!" She took great delight in that fact. She had never expressed an interest in any other man. Her love for her husband would last her lifetime.

Fridays were special nights for the children, especially when Gram's younger sister Liz drove up with her husband, Gerhard. He was a tall, stately, railroad man who said very little but instead loved to sit and work crossword puzzles. When the children arrived and the music was turned up, however, no one sat still for long. They spent the evening dancing, singing, and having a ball.

✠   ✠   ✠

One particular Friday marked the last time Gram would ever drive the children down Schooley's Mountain Road. We were made uneasily aware that there were changes taking place in this wonder-ful, capable woman. I recall the episode well, and had I not been in the car that night I would not have understood the jeopardy the children would be in when riding in the car with Gram.

She pulled out of our driveway and started down the moun-tain. The car built up speed, and Gram did not even attempt to slow down for the curve ahead.

"Careful, Gram," I said. We continued to build momentum and neared the next curve. My calm gave way to sheer terror.

"Grandma, slow down. Put on your brakes!" I shouted.

She did not. She would not. We were flying. Somehow we made it to the bottom without incident. Noticeably shaken, I asked her why she hadn't slowed down.

"I can go from the top of the mountain to the bottom without ever touching my brakes. It saves on my brakes, you know."

It was then that I began to wonder about Grandma. It was very much in character for her to be concerned about saving her brakes—she never wasted anything. Yet to risk her life and the lives of her great-grandchildren was definitely not in character, and it frightened me. I knew that we would have to start doing some things differently.

✠   ✠   ✠

Little did we know that these alarming signs were only the begin-ning of a rapid deterioration of her mind and reason—a degener-ation caused by Alzheimer's disease.

2

I often stood at the picture window of our home on Schooley's Mountain, counting the heads of children. They could usually be spotted perched on a gnarled branch of a grand, old apple tree or swinging on the rope hung from one of its taller limbs. If I had to look up any higher, I would drop whatever I was doing and run outside. The yard was filled with many great climbing trees, and the boys were convinced they were great climbers—at least until they reached the top of the tree.

"Christopher Walsh! What are you doing up there?"

Chris, then eight years old, had climbed almost to the top of a very tall pine tree—not a good climbing tree. He was in a very precarious position.

"I thought I could get down, Mommy, but I can't!" came his timid reply. I proceeded to direct him as to where to place his feet and which branch to hold tightly. It was a tense situation—and it took some time—but he made it down safely. The moment his feet were firmly planted on the earth, I lost my calm demeanor.

Now as I again stood looking out over the familiar countryside alive in sumptuous spring array, I couldn't help but sigh. I would miss this chapter in our lives.

I gazed up at the tree house nearly hidden by the apple tree's lush, pink blossoms. Ed and the boys had spent days hammering and sawing, constructing what turned out to be a favorite spot for each of us. On many pleasant summer evenings, Ed would surround himself with pillows and children and read through the Chronicles of Narnia by C. S. Lewis. Only the dusk and the chirping of crickets could convince them that it was time to come down.

But prodded by the impending need for a new roof, we began to think about moving. There was much to consider.

Jamie would soon be entering high school, and our desire was to continue sending him, along with our other children, to a private Christian school. The only schools that went up through twelfth grade were located at least an hour away. The thought of carpooling that distance for many years to come was overwhelming. We located a school in Pennsylvania that taught through twelfth grade and began our search there.

Realizing that Gram and Flip, now nearing eighty, would be left alone and unable to maintain their home and property, we offered to move them along with us. There were no other close relatives in the area.

They were delighted.

We discussed the future. Our hope was to care for them for the rest of their lives.

"Oh, Gram, I'd never put you in a nursing home, you can be sure of that," Ed said confidently. He knew how much she loathed the idea. After all the sacrifices she had made for him over the years, how could he ever think of it. For my part, I could not in my wildest dreams imagine this capable, independent woman ever needing to be cared for. In my mind, she would probably live to be a hundred and end up taking care of all of us.

Since we would need a house large enough to accommodate our growing clan, a cross over the border into Pennsylvania made a significant difference in what we could afford. We were able to get more house for our money, and taxes were considerably lower. The Pennsylvania border was only forty minutes from our house on Schooley's Mountain.

After months of searching, an ad caught my eye. This one seemed just right.

Mother-daughter log home. Five bedrooms, stone fireplace, country setting, charming.

The next day we drove to Pennsylvania. We arrived at the house before the owners and had a few minutes to look around. We walked up to the deck that ran the full length of the house in the backyard, surveying the countryside. It was a far different picture than the one to which I had grown accustomed at our house on Schooley's Mountain. This house was in a neighborhood, though the setting was very secluded and surrounded by woods. When we peered through the windows, we were hopelessly smitten.

The place had such character. A massive stone fireplace filled one corner of the room. The cedar logs of the roof cast a mellow, amber hue over the open expanse, and to our delight, a twisted oak tree served as a support at the center. It was such a storybook atmosphere that I could almost picture a dwarf or two appearing from the woodwork. When the owners drove up, we greeted them with anticipation. They knew we were already sold.

As they escorted us through the house, we felt sure that it would be perfect for us. The main house was rustic, as we liked it. The downstairs apartment was more contemporary, as Gram and Flip were accustomed to.

Storybook indeed—yet the story that would unfold there in the following years would be far from a fairy tale.

✠   ✠   ✠

Grandma's house sold quickly. As in any move, there were plenty of unexpected surprises. Gram's property needed a new septic system and a new well. A slow leak under one of the bedroom floors had destroyed the flooring. It had to be torn up, replaced, and recarpeted. Soon after the closing of the sale on her house, the mortgage on the new house fell through. It was an unsettling time. What if we couldn't get a mortgage? Gram's house had already sold. I had visions of us all living huddled beneath our old, leaky farmhouse roof, clutching pots and pans.

Then came a big surprise! Ed walked in one night and announced, "When the phone rings, answer it, 'Walsh Estimating Service'. I'm on my own!"

Ed had been in construction since early in our marriage. He started out with a maintenance crew picking up debris on worksites, moved up to the position of foreman, and eventually became the estimator and vice president of a large paving company. After several years, problems developed within the business. He had, at times, seriously considered going into business for himself—now the decision had been made.

"I'm going to provide an estimating service for construction companies all over the country, companies who don't have their own in-house estimator, or for those simply overloaded with work. Everything will be shipped overnight, so it doesn't matter where they are located."

His years of estimating experience would provide the knowledge and expertise to take on jobs ranging from schools and shopping centers to bridges and major landfills.

His first purchase was a computerized take-off system, valued at $20,000. I wasn't sure if this was a step of faith or a step off a cliff. With this, he assured me, he could provide contractors with accurate quantities and three-dimensional views of their projects, along with costs for excavation, clearing, underground utilities, curbs, paving, and landscaping.

At the end of Walsh Estimating's first week, we were encouraged. Ed's reputation followed him, and customers trusted him. His first paycheck was promising. How we ever secured a mortgage, having started a business only weeks earlier, I will never know.

"Mary, did I tell you that Fred offered one of his trucks to move us? A forty-five-foot box trailer! Do you think that will be big enough?" he laughed.

"It had better be! We should get rid of a lot of stuff at the moving sale Saturday. The ad is in tonight's paper."

✠   ✠   ✠

When we arrived at Gram's house Saturday morning, she met us
with her usual open arms and delightful greeting.

"Enter family!"

As we approached the open door, Ed slipped his arm around
my waist, pretending to whisper in my ear as he pointed to his
grandmother.

"Mary, if you look half as good as Gram when you're eighty,
I'll be happy!"

There she stood with her extended arm holding the screen
door open, her silky blouse neatly tucked into her white slacks, a
wide leather belt accentuating her tiny waist. She stood so tall and
carried herself so graciously, you would assume her to be taller
than the 5'4" she was. She accepted the compliment with a smile.

"Are you ready for the big sale, Gram?" Ed asked as he hugged
her affectionately. He stepped back from her as he noticed a large
Band-Aid stretched across the bridge of her nose.

"What happened to your nose, Gram?"

"Oh, it's nothing, darling. I just took care of something this
morning. It's fine."

Ed and I looked at one another, realizing that she had, in fact,
performed minor surgery. There had been a large growth on her
nose, about the size of an eraser tip. To remove it would require
skill and experience. We had encouraged her to make an appointment, but it was too late for that now. She had taken care of it
herself—with a razor knife.

The very thought sent a chill through my body. The sensation
took me back to that stunned moment at the bottom of Schooley's
Mountain, following the wild ride without brakes. I was unsettled,
and I knew Ed felt as I did.

"Come in and have some coffee. Sister and I just made some
bread. Sit down and have a piece!"

She didn't need to ask again. The delicious aroma of coffee
mingled with that of warm cinnamon drew us to the kitchen. Gram
always made cinnamon bread along with her white bread, and it
tasted every bit as good as it smelled.

"Don't forget to take a loaf home with you, darling," she insisted.

This would be a busy morning, so her usual baking agenda of bread, apple pies, and sometimes a cake, would have to be postponed. Though we could have sat all morning eating bread and drinking coffee, there was work to be done.

It was a sale to end all sales. Cars parked along the road and filled up the long driveway leading to Grandma's house. They pulled away, loaded with boxes and bags filled with toys, clothing, tools, yarn—you name it. Prices were cheap.

Gram was in rare form. She had never hosted a garage sale but had plenty of department store sales experience. It came in handy.

She began advertising the items for sale and having a ball. "Wouldn't you like to buy this lovely lamp? Look at the lampshade." She displayed it as she walked, and customers watched with curiosity. It became more of an auction than a garage sale. Everything was sold or given away.

Despite all we had gotten rid of, we still filled the entire forty-five-foot box trailer. We moved out, working around Ed, who stayed at his desk, bringing in business. We thought we would have to carry him out at the end. All that remained in the house was the telephone.

New job, new state, new home, along with Gram and Flip—we were on our way!

✢   ✢   ✢

I was elected to drive. The car was packed—eight of us plus the dog. The truck, loaded with the contents of two houses, followed close behind.

"If you look real close and use your imagination, you can see the profiles of the Delaware Indians on the face of those cliffs up there," I told the children. We drove through the Delaware Water Gap and approached the border between New Jersey and Pennsylvania. "At least that's what my brother Bruce once told me." Bruce had lived in the Pocono Mountains for several years. We would now be neighbors.

My daughter, Dawn, squinted her eyes and leaned way back to catch a glimpse.

"Hey, Mom! What does that sign mean?" Chris asked, obviously confused.

"What did it say, Chris?"

"It says 'Welcome to Pennsylvania. America Starts Here!'"

"Gee, I don't know, hon. I always thought I was part of America when I lived in New Jersey."

My first impression of the Delaware Water Gap was that it was wild. The road meandered between the Delaware River and the jutting rock faces towering above. With each turn, the scenery changed dramatically, rock slides to our right, cliffs and sheer rock faces to our left. The powerful scenery lured my eyes from the road, which required every bit of my attention.

"The Appalachian Trail cuts through this mountain. We'll have to go up there sometime!" Ed said with anticipation.

I felt uneasy. From my perspective, it looked as if we would need ropes and hooks to hike up there. I enjoyed hiking in the woods, but I had heard that these woods were filled with black bears. I remembered all too well the numerous snakes I encountered as a young girl vacationing in Pennsylvania.

I never would have dreamed that this wild, extraordinary piece of God's creation would become a familiar and special place to me during the difficult years ahead.

✠   ✠   ✠

We settled into our new home over the next several weeks. Flip seemed very content in the new downstairs apartment, but Gram, although happy with the arrangement, was noticeably confused. She would come upstairs and into our bedroom and ask if it was her living room. We would take her down and show her the living room. Then she would come up with a picture to hang in "her" living room or her twin-sized bedspread for the queen-sized bed in our room.

"Gram, it's much too small for the bed," I'd say as I spread it out to show her.

"No, it's the one for that bed," she'd insist.

"It will fit your bed downstairs. I'll show you." We would go down, and I'd put the bedspread neatly on her bed. She seemed satisfied, but within a short time she would be back upstairs with it, march into the bedroom, and attempt to fit it on the bed once again.

Within a short time she settled down and appeared to be very much at home. Concerned, we scheduled a doctor's appointment to determine the cause of her confusion. Her doctor sent her for a brain scan. He told us that she was showing very early signs of dementia. Although he suspected Alzheimer's disease, it was too early to determine definitively. Time would tell.

Soon her singing began. Gram had a lovely singing voice. Each new great-grandchild was welcomed into her home and arms with the gentlest of lullabys.

"Let me take the little bunny, darling," she would insist. She'd wrap a blanket around the fussing baby and begin to stroll the floors, firmly patting their backs—all the while singing softly.

"Lullaby and goodnight."

She would continue, stringing along one melody after another.

"Away in a manger no crib for a bed, the little Lord Jesus," she would sing.

Although there were no crying infants to console after the move, Gram seemed content to sing all the time. Her singing began to take on an increase in volume that allowed us to hear it from every room in the house. We would hear her first thing in the morning.

"East side, west side, all around the town."

"Suzie O'Grady."

"London Bridge is falling down."

"All around the Mulberry bush, the monkey chased the weasel, that's the way the money goes, *POP* goes the weasel!"

She would sing while she was rolling her pie crust, while she was doing dishes, while dusting or knitting. It became the back-ground music in the Walsh home.

She and Flip continued preparing meals, and the children often ate dinner downstairs with them. On those occasions when Ed and I would go out for the evening, she assured us they would be taken care of. One such evening, as we prepared to leave, I smelled the distinct aroma of baking fish coming from the downstairs kitchen.

"I guess your grandmother is making fish for dinner," I said to Ed as I grabbed my coat. "I hope the kids will eat it. They're not crazy about fish."

We returned home later that evening and could still detect a slight fish aroma.

"Hi, Gram, we're home. I guess you had fish for dinner. Did the kids eat it?" Ed asked.

"Fish? We didn't have fish. We had chicken à la king," she corrected.

"Why do I smell fish?" he asked, walking toward the kitchen.

"I don't know, darling."

We looked over at Jamie, who was rolling his eyes and motioning for us to come into the next room. "We had fish à la king tonight," he whispered. "Gram used fish instead of chicken! It was disgusting!"

We felt bad and, upon investigation, found that she had indeed substituted fish unknowingly for chicken—and the children, not wishing to hurt her feelings, had eaten it all.

God bless them.

✠   ✠   ✠

We no longer allowed the children to ride in the car with Gram, having once watched her pull a U-turn in front of a huge dump truck, causing the driver to literally stand on his brakes in order to stop in time. The time had come—we knew we would have to take away her keys. This small action on our part was more than difficult to accomplish, it was almost impossible. Ed first attempted reasoning with her.

"Gram, do you realize that in the past year and a half you have been involved in four accidents?"

"And I suppose you think that they were all my fault?" she demanded indignantly, hands firmly planted on her hips.

"Gram, all four cars were standing still!" he explained.

"Do you think I'm a bad driver, Margaretta? How about you, Mary?"

We would try our best to be tactful, but she would take it as a personal affront.

"You're all against me!"

Gram very reluctantly handed over her keys, but she never stopped trying to drive. No matter who was at the wheel, she was at the helm. As her mind continued to deteriorate, her instructions became more absurd and increasingly emphatic. I'm a patient person, but there were many times I was tempted to abandon the car.

"Take it, darling!" she would insist as I was waiting to pull out into traffic. It was often at a busy intersection. I would wait until it was safe.

"I said, take it, darling!"

"Gram, if I take it we will be under that truck!"

"If you take it, they will just have to wait," she assured me.

Those minutes seemed like hours and she would inevitably end up angry and insulted.

She was determined to maintain the control she always had. Her need to control matters impacted everyone in the months ahead. Her strength—both physical and mental—was gradually diminishing, and she fought hard to hold on to it.

$\mathscr{A}$MERICA $\mathscr{S}$TARTS $\mathscr{H}$ERE

$\mathscr{T}$he world outside our wonderful, new log house held many surprises.

We learned quickly to identify natives. It wasn't their dialect or their distinguishing dress that gave them away—it was their bumper stickers. Visit the Poconos . . . then go home! or If you don't like it, take I-80 East! or I'm not a tourist, I'm an armed native! A more recent one, by far the best, If there's a tourist season, why can't we shoot 'em? These bumper stickers gave new meaning to the word *native.*

"Where are you from?" asked the gentleman in the grocery store as he packed my numerous bags of groceries. Until that moment we had been having a nice conversation, discussing a recent bear sighting and the spectacular weather. My answer put an end to that cordiality.

"I'm from New Jersey."

You would think by the expression on his face that I had lit a foul-smelling smoke bomb.

"You people have ruined this place!" he said with a clenched jaw. "This used to be a nice place to live, but it's not the same now . . . the traffic . . . you city people."

His was a commonly held sentiment in these parts. Come to think of it, we never had received a visit from the Welcome Wagon since moving in. I assumed, perhaps, they were so booked up with the influx of new residents that they were behind schedule.

I was beginning to understand, yet I was taken back by his outrage and was a little embarrassed.

"That will be $124.00," said the woman at the register.

I carefully counted out the money.

"Gee, I hope you don't mind taking this money," I said as sheepishly as I could, "me coming from New Jersey."

He continued to stew as I headed toward the door with my overloaded shopping cart.

It appeared to me that a considerable portion of the tourists came for a visit, returned home, packed up, and moved in. Many families came from the cities of New York and New Jersey. I think they hoped to establish a home in the country and escape urban problems.

☩   ☩   ☩

The wonderful weather we had talked about was indeed wonderful. And it soon made me forget the grocery clerk's surliness.

Summer was now at hand.

My cart was loaded with summer supplies—watermelon, paper plates, Popsicles. In a few short days the children would be home for summer vacation.

Friends and I had concluded that the first days of summer were always the most traumatic. The first week was often ushered in by an event—such as a trip to the emergency room for stitches.

I looked forward to my children being home for the summer with great anticipation. As they got older, that joy gradually turned to trepidation.

From the time Jamie and Chris could talk, they would come up with the most ingenious ways to entertain themselves. They kept me on the edge of my seat. Jamie was the mastermind and Chris would do just about anything his big brother told him to.

How well I recall the muffled scream emanating from the dryer one muggy summer morning. Knowing I hadn't started any laundry, I yanked the door open in time to catch three-year-old

Christopher as he tumbled out onto the floor. Jamie was standing close by, observing.

"Christopher, what were you doing in the dryer?" I asked. I was relieved he wasn't hurt, but angry he had been in such an absurd predicament in the first place.

"I accidentally fell into the dryer!" he whined looking up at me with those winsome, brown eyes, shaking his head of red ringlets alive with static.

"And I accidentally turned it on!" Jamie assured me as the older and wiser one.

They loved to camp out and make forts, and our new home, surrounded by woods on three sides, afforded them great opportunity. Jamie once constructed an impressive fort using fallen trees and large vinyl tarps and was anxious to spend the night in it. I was concerned about an enormous bear that had been spotted in our neighborhood.

(I was not afraid of bears—but this was a very big bear.)

"Remember, Jamie, I'll keep a light on near the house in case you want to come in during the night," I assured him.

"Oh, Mom, that's silly. I'm not afraid. I'll see you in the morning!"

Gram had been listening to our conversation. Over the past few weeks, she had become increasingly anxious concerning the whereabouts of the children.

"Mary, are they all home? Where are they? Shouldn't we go look for them?"

When she overheard my conversation with Jamie, she became alarmed.

"Where is he going, Mary?" she asked.

"Jamie is camping out tonight, Gram," I replied.

"Outside? In the woods?" she asked in obvious disapproval.

"He'll be fine, Gram. Edward said it's OK," I assured her. Often just hearing the name Edward would calm her fears. If it was OK with Edward, it was OK with her.

Yet she still seemed agitated.

The following morning I thought I heard someone yelling behind the house.

"Eddie, did you hear that?" I asked, remembering that Jamie was in the woods.

"It sounds like Flip!"

We ran out the back door. Flip was on the hill below, hovering over someone on the ground. All I could envision was that monstrous black bear.

"Flip, what happened?" Eddie yelled.

"It's Gramma! She wouldn't listen. She went to look for Jamie in the woods. I told her he was fine, but she wouldn't listen!"

Gram had gotten dressed, put on her flimsy bedroom slippers, and headed out the back door. The hill behind the house was steep and slick with the morning dew. Gram immediately slipped down the incline, landing flat on her back.

At the hospital they determined she had fractured her spine. She was in tremendous pain and for weeks could only recline on the couch.

Jamie, however, was not in the woods that night. He had changed his mind not long after dark. Perhaps he heard that bear—but he wouldn't tell me. He had been snugly tucked in his own bed the entire time.

☩   ☩   ☩

The fort became a meeting place for neighboring children. There were always kids at the door—often equipped with their dads' favorite tools—anxious to go work on the fort.

Alan, a young neighbor boy, appeared at the door.

"Mom, can I show Alan the fort?" David asked.

"OK, hon, but come right back—dinner is almost ready."

Flip was carrying salads out to the picnic table. I was grilling hamburgers and hot dogs as the smoke chased me around the grill. "These are ready! You can call everyone to dinner, Dawn!"

Within a matter of seconds, Jamie came running up to the deck yelling "Fire! The woods are on fire!"

Running toward the woods, we could see the fort was ablaze.

"Oh, Lord!" I yelled. "David is at the fort!"

We ran ahead as people filled buckets of water. I watched as the plastic tarp melted in the blaze of fire and fell heavily to the ground below. I was horrified. When we reached the fort, we discovered, thankfully, that David was not inside. But he was nowhere to be found. We searched everywhere.

We found him hiding in the mower shed, terrified to come out. He burst out crying. He was afraid we would be angry with him. If only he knew how absolutely thrilled we were to see that little freckled face.

I learned later that Alan had taken a box of matches from the grill. On the way to the fort, David watched as Alan attempted to set plants in the woods on fire. When they got to the fort, he told David, "Stand inside and light the tarp. I want to see what happens." The boy ran home, and David escaped. That evening, I spoke with the boy's father and told him of the near tragedy. He did not appear to be surprised or concerned.

As I returned home, I pondered all that had happened. The image of that blazing, molten plastic tarp falling to the ground was branded in my memory. It made me realize how much we had to be thankful for, and how drastically our lives could have been changed in an instant.

Rising early in our new home on quiet summer mornings brought its own rewards. I took my Bible and a cup of coffee out on the deck and enjoyed a few peaceful moments.

The delicate summer breeze whispered hints of days gone by—the simple pleasures of being a child—slipping on a new pair of sneakers and pulling my hair back into a ponytail. Some of my favorite memories are of long, sunny summer days. I'd head for the backyard of our family home in New Jersey, the grass still wet with the morning dew, to be the first one on the swing. I'd listen to the birds conversing in the treetops. They were as delighted with the new day as I was.

I longed to catch a glimpse of a stunning red bird with black wings, the Scarlet Tanager. Not just any Scarlet Tanager, but one we called by name—Flair. My big brother Bruce had found the injured bird hobbling in the grass. He carried him home in a shoebox, and the bird quickly became a part of our family.

Each morning we would wait at the bus stop, Flair perched on top of Bruce's head. The busdriver, Mr. Pickle, would throw open the bus door, unable to contain his obvious delight. The sight made his day. Flair would spend each day with Bruce in class, content to sit on his shoulder and watch him work. This became his routine for weeks to come.

As much as we wanted to keep Flair, we knew he must eventually learn to fly again. We would each take a turn running through the yard with him perched on our hands, always secretly relieved he was not quite ready to take off.

One day my brother Jeff took his turn, and Flair was off, flying to the top of a nearby tree.

"He's flying! Flair can fly!" Jeff yelled. Bruce came running. He was sad that he was not the one to see him off.

We looked up into the dense treetop and could see Flair gazing hesitantly toward the sky, then down on us. He made his choice, but we were sad. Such a wild and independent bird, so dependent on us for a time and then gone. Although we looked for him often after that, we never saw him again.

On the swing—legs pumping, eyes closed—I'd lean way back. My eyes would open, sizing up the morning sky. Would it be a swimming day or a fishing day? Maybe both.

Swimming was such an important part of summer—to me it *was* summer! Living between neighbors who owned pools could be torture. The days you were not invited to swim were the hottest and longest of all. What lengths we would go to just to get cooled off!

When I was six, my brother Jeff surprised us with a pool of our own. He labored all morning, digging deep into the dirt and clay of our backyard, spurred on by the vision of a refreshing dip in the hot afternoon.

"Get your bathing suits, girls! Come and take a swim," he said. He was very proud of his accomplishment.

My friend Suzanne wasn't nearly as eager as I. Jeff's pool was about three feet square and three feet deep. It was not sparkling blue as were the neighbors' pools; it was murky brown.

But it was a hot day.

I ran inside the house and discovered, to my great disappointment, my bathing suit at the bottom of a hamper of dirty clothes. I reappeared moments later, however, in my underwear. At six years old, it made little difference to me or anyone else.

Suzanne laughed at the sight of me running toward the "pool."

"You're crazy, Mamie," her older sister, Nancy, yelled, rolling her eyes. Nancy often rolled her eyes at moments such as this. I was the one willing to venture out where no one else dared.

Plunging into water that looked and felt like pea soup, my excitement quickly curtailed. Within minutes there was no water in the pool at all. All that was left was a muddy hole.

"We can fill it again!" assured Jeff, yet the water seemed to disappear as quickly as he replenished it.

It was a short-lived, muddy, but memorable swim.

✠   ✠   ✠

My pleasant childhood memories disappeared in an instant. I heard a frantic call from the backyard and could tell by the urgency in Flip's voice that Grandma was involved. Leaning over the railing, I caught a glimpse of Grandma tugging at some vines that hung from a massive pine tree near the back door. Within seconds, I was down the stairs and in the backyard.

"She will not give me the knife! I've tried to get it from her," Flip cried out as they struggled.

Not only was Grandma clutching the largest and sharpest butcher's knife we owned, she was standing on a hill soaked with the morning dew, again wearing flimsy bedroom slippers.

"I must remove these ugly things," she insisted, wrapping one hand around the inch-thick vine and sawing vigorously with the other.

"Grandma, please give me the knife and come back inside," I coaxed. She continued to saw.

"No, I must remove them."

I knew very well that there was no way she would willingly surrender that knife. Flip restrained her by the waist as I grabbed her wrist, squeezing it tightly until she released the knife.

We dragged her into the house. She sat for a few moments in her chair but was soon on her feet again, headed for the sliding glass door.

"My, look at those ugly vines on that tree," she said as if discovering them for the first time. "Margaretta, get me a knife," she insisted. The knives were put up, hidden, but she began to look for them.

In a moment, all was calm in the downstairs apartment.

✠   ✠   ✠

At the front door was our young neighbor boy with blond hair and bright eyes.

"Is Jamie home? I brought my ropes. Jamie told me he'd teach me how to rappel."

"Oh, he did, did he?" I answered. "What's your name?"

"Eric. I live around the corner."

My first impression of Eric was that of a bright, very inquisitive, just plain likable boy.

But rappelling?

It was a word Jamie had only recently introduced me to.

"It's completely safe, Mom. You just have to know what you're doing."

I had often heard those reassuring words in his short fourteen years. I had heard them broadcast from the top of the tallest tree in the yard and from ten feet off the ground straddling a bike over a jump. From the time Jamie was a toddler, tearing from room to room and around corners on two wheels of his four-wheeled walker, Ed and I knew we were in for an adventure. Jamie seemed to be most comfortable with a helmet on his head and wheels on his feet—but those wheels had to be off the ground and moving fast. To my motherly dismay, rappelling was his latest intrigue.

Later that afternoon I was introduced to a certain type of rappelling—bungled rappelling.

I heard a commotion out on the back deck and realized that all four of my children were out there, plus some neighbors. Something unusual seemed about to take place. I made it outside just in time to catch Jamie securing a climbing rope to a log extending from one corner of the house, two stories up. Eric was taking in every maneuver.

"Wait a minute, guys. What do you think you're doing?" I inquired.

"Mom, it's perfectly safe."

"Safe or not, we are not going to be rappelling off the house."

He persuaded me to allow him to demonstrate just how safe it really was. He harnessed himself quickly, as if this was something at which he had become quite proficient, grabbed the rope, and very smoothly descended to the grass below. He returned up the steps with another bright idea.

"Come here, Mom, put this harness on and see for yourself— it's perfectly safe."

"Jamie, I'm really not interested in rappelling."

"Oh, come on, Mrs. Walsh, you can do it!" Eric prodded.

Before I could refuse again, I found myself fastened securely into the harness with clear instructions about which rope to hold tightly and which to release.

The descent was smooth, my feet landing firmly on the ground. We all laughed. Convinced that they would survive this unharmed, I allowed Eric one turn also.

"OK, now, let's get the ropes up and away."

"But Mom, I never get a turn at anything," came surprisingly from my daughter, Dawn, now ten years old.

"Oh, Dawn, I don't know. Something might happen. You could get hurt," I said cautiously.

"Now, Mom, you watched how Eric and I got down. What could possibly go wrong?" Jamie campaigned.

"The only way I will allow it is if I go down below—just in case," which I did. Jamie helped Dawn into the harness.

"Now, when I tell you, Dawn, you hold on to this rope and release it a little at a time as you go down. It's simple!" Jamie coached.

I stood below, looking up with my arms raised high, not quite believing I had been talked into this. Down she came several feet— but her thrill was short lived. She stopped with a jolt and a scream.

"Help me, Mommy!" she screamed.

Her beautiful, long, dark hair had gotten caught in the metal connector, and she could not move up or down. If she moved the slightest bit, her scalp was pulled so that you could see it bulging. Any move in either direction would have torn out her hair. She was down far enough that I could reach my arms up and support her weight, but this did not solve the problem.

"Jamie, get a ladder! Quick, get scissors! Do something!"

"She's fine, Mom." he assured me.

"Hurry!"

Dawn's pitiful pleas kept me supporting her weight.

I could see Grandma watching me through the downstairs window, yet she seemed to be looking through me. She had no idea what was going on. The time was not long past when she would have been right there to take charge of the situation.

Jamie got a chair and managed to release the metal connector. He cut a small amount of the hair that had been caught, and we got her down. Dawn suffered only from a very sore scalp for several days.

"OK, guys, the ropes come down. No more rappelling, and I don't want to hear any more about it!"

They obeyed. I would not hear any more about rappelling— until later on that summer.

$\mathscr{A}$RE $\mathscr{W}$E $\mathscr{H}$AVING $\mathscr{F}$UN $\mathscr{Y}$ET?   5

$\mathscr{T}$here is a well-guarded secret in the Poconos, one privy only to the natives and those who live there long enough to discover it: how to get around the horrendous weekend traffic. I found there was a local understanding—if a tourist with a New Jersey or New York license plate stopped to ask for a shortcut around traffic, they were simply told no. The funny thing was, it was a friend of mine, also from New Jersey, who told me this.

"But, you tell them the shortcuts, don't you?" I asked.

"Of course not," she laughed.

One Saturday (before we had been clued in to this guarded, inside information), we had been sitting for about thirty minutes in bumper-to-bumper traffic when Ed said, "Hon, why don't you and Jamie get together and plan a little vacation for the family, maybe to the shore? Soon, I'll be so swamped with work, I won't be able to leave."

"Sounds great, Dad!" Jamie chimed in.

"You know," Ed continued, "we may not be able to leave Gram alone with Flip for much longer. She may soon become too much for Flip to handle. Wouldn't you like to take a vacation?"

Vacation evokes in me somewhat the same feeling as the word *dentist* does for other people. You pay all that money and you really don't have much fun. I would actually prefer the dentist—at least I always know what to expect when I sit in that chair.

I can trace my vacation cynicism back to my childhood.

My dad prepared us for our vacations. He went far beyond the physical preparations. Whether it was to a museum or a ferry ride around Manhattan, we knew we were in for a great time. His love for history was contagious. If our destination was an historical sight, he would stop the car and let his stories take us back in time until we believed we were there! We could see Jenny jumping off the cliff to escape an attacking Indian, or soldiers breathing their last out on the battlefields.

Preparations for our first camping trip as a family were almost as exciting as the actual trip. My six brothers and I were taken to a large military surplus store. Each of us was equipped with a comfy, flannel-lined sleeping bag, a duffel bag, a whistle, a compass, a flashlight, and a sailor's cap. We took collapsible canvas water buckets and even a portable toilet with a curtain for the utmost privacy. All we had to do was dig the hole.

However, as well planned as our trips may have been, we found we could not always fully prepare for the unexpected.

Dad was always proud to have the family together, crowded into the station wagon, along with the family dog. Our basset hound, Boots, accompanied us on these trips, claiming his spot behind the driver's seat. He'd position his stubby hind legs on the edge of the backseat and drop a paw over Dad's shoulder. Hanging his head out the window, he'd let his long, pendulous ears flap in the breeze. He would rest his head on Dad's shoulder when the ride became wearisome.

"How many kids have you got there?" attendants would inquire curiously as we stopped for gas.

"Seven! Six boys and one girl!" he'd reply.

"She must be treated like a queen," they'd respond.

It is remarkable how many times I heard that growing up. I guess it was, in fact, true. Taking my place in the middle of six boys, with the understanding that any mistreatment of the one daughter would result in six unhappy boys, made me feel like a princess in a strong fortress.

I'm sure my special position was resented at times—especially on nights when Dad found an interesting movie on television. I would sit up on his lap eating popcorn.

"Now, you boys go to bed! We're downstairs eating popcorn."

They loved that, I'm sure.

We were well equipped for our vacations, no doubt, but not totally prepared. On our first family camping trip there was a violent storm that threatened to relocate our enormous tent in the middle of the night. I can still see my dad leaning the weight of his entire body against the massive wooden center pole in an attempt to keep it standing. The large canvas tarp that had been attached to the pole at the peak of the tent was being hoisted by the wind. Lightning flashes revealed our frightened faces as we sat clutching pots and pans to catch the dripping water.

Thoroughly exhausted from the night, we left the soggy campsite for a sightseeing drive the following morning.

The day was damp and chilly and it actually felt good to be back in the crowded station wagon—dog and all. Dad still had his sailor's cap on and his pipe in his mouth, clenched securely between his teeth. He was no doubt a bit shaken by the storm but didn't show it. He was still on vacation.

"Well, wait a minute! We've got to stop up ahead. We're at the Ausable Chasm!" There was that whisper of suspense in his voice as he read from a travel brochure:

> Sheer walls of rock rise some 200 feet above the rushing waters of the Ausable River. A tour of the chasm includes a short hike on dangling suspension bridges and winding walkways, past plunging waterfalls and raging rapids, culminating in a boat ride through the swirling waters.

We received a few instructions. I was to keep the dog on his leash, Mom had my youngest brother, Chris, close by her side. Bruce, Jeff, little Wally, and Carl were to follow Dad. We climbed carefully down some boulders, wet and slick with moss—not an easy feat for a basset hound. We could hear the deafening roar of the mighty rapids, rushing furiously from the previous night's storm. Soon we could see for ourselves why Dad had made the stop.

It was breathtaking!

As we stood together looking warily down into the chasm, I recall my dad's words, "I seriously doubt a man could fall in there and come out alive. Let's head back."

With that, he turned to leave. Seconds later, my brother Bruce, who had been mesmerized by the water, was falling head-long down into the rapids. It was one of those moments when you are awakened with a jolt from a terrible dream, so relieved—but this was no dream.

"Bruce fell in!" I screamed.

Without a moment's hesitation, Dad made his way to the edge and jumped in. I could see Bruce's arms flailing out of the water as he was tossed around and pulled under by the rapids. Within seconds, my mother made her way to the edge, jumped in, and was pulled down the river as well. I grabbed as many little hands as I could and walked along the chasm, hoping to see all three, remembering all too well my Dad's ominous words. Would they come out alive?

What a wonderful sight it was to see my dad, sailor cap still on his head, and—I kid you not—pipe in his mouth, standing beyond the rapids in an alcove of rocks, embracing Bruce and Mom.

It was a very tearful, thankful, crowded ride back to camp. Bruce cried the loudest, however. Thankful, yes, that he had not lost his life, but also mourning a comparable tragedy to him—he had lost his harmonica.

We sat quietly at the picnic table in the stillness of evening, humbled by the day.

"Do you see the frail little mantle in this lantern?" Dad asked. We gazed in to see the delicate mantle providing the only light in the campsite.

"That is how frail our life is. In one second, it can be taken away!"

We were dirty. We were tired. We were sick of being on vacation. But the following morning we filed into the nearest church we could find, just to say "thank you" that we would all be heading home.

✠   ✠   ✠

My dad wrote the following letter to his parents in 1964 following our family camping vacation and the memorable incident at the Ausable Chasm. It was discovered long after the completion of this chapter, in fact a year after my dad died. I had never seen the letter before, and it was so interesting for me to read it and see how much I remembered of that day, though I was so young. It is also further evidence as to why the word vacation brings on a near panic attack and why my teacher thought I was telling tales when I turned in my "What I Did on My Summer Vacation" essay.

Dear Folks:

I told you I would write about Bruce and our vacation. So here goes.

We really couldn't afford a vacation, but with the recent disturbance on my job and a dozen other things that seemed overwhelming, we knew that we had to get away somehow. Naturally the cheapest way was to camp—and we also like it. A friend of mine at the office suggested we go to Lake George and rent an island. This sounded good to me because one thing I needed was to really get away.

We got to Lake George having car trouble all the way, but not serious enough to stop us, and we found out quick enough the "island idea" was both impractical and too hazardous for a family such as ours. We would have to rent a power boat which was unbelievably expensive to get to an island three miles out in the lake—and it was silly to think of transporting the amount of equipment and family we have out—and then to wish for a fast return in case a storm should come up, etc.

But luck was with us. About twenty-five miles north, still

on Lake George, and six miles below Ticonderoga, we settled into the nicest campsite out of 250 (we thought it was the nicest and still do), a two-minute walk up from the lake, and for $1.25 per day we had it made. This was at Roger's Rock, a historic mountain of the Revolutionary War period, with pine trees a hundred feet tall and little red squirrels throwing butternuts down on us every morning. It was really great. The nights were cold but the days were fine and the swimming refreshing.

Then the car went bad. Still our good luck held out. I found a fine mechanic who fixed the front end with a new part for ten dollars that had been quoted here at home for seventy-five. This knocked the morning for me. But there was still trouble. We went back and found that a new left-rear wheel bearing was needed badly. That took the next afternoon and another ten dollars. Thinking that everything was undoubtedly fit as a fiddle and with the following after-noon rainy and unpleasant around the camp, I decided to take the kids to Fort Ticonderoga. We got there but that was about all. I ended up with the Dodge place in Ticonderoga and, again, found a really fine mechanic. He said to take it on back and made a date for me the next morning early. I was there. He hoisted it up in the air and found that the emergency brake was loose and that the driveshaft had about a quarter inch play in it. Seemed logical that this was certainly the trouble, the grabbing that I had felt in the back end. He then started going over the engine and tuning it up from one end to the other. I figured it was all to the good since the major troubles were fixed and I was looking at the old wagon as if it were a new car. I was there for nine hours. It cost me fifty dollars and felt wonderful on the ride back to camp. Believe me, I was really thrilled!

That evening, we had a fine time with another family, a police commissioner from our area at home, until about ten o'clock—when Jean suddenly got a bug in her ear! Away we went with all the kids in the car, back to Ticonderoga to look for a doctor. But we didn't get there! The car stopped dead about two miles out in the country. I used a farmer's phone and located the mechanic who came scampering out over the hills in his little Volkswagen, lifted the hood, and found a wire broken off the distributor. Bring it into the shop tomorrow morning and we'll fix it right, thank you, and off we went. We got the doctor to come to his office and he rinsed Jean's ear out—but the bug had flown by this time. I paid him four dollars, and we went back to camp. And on the way, the old rear-end trouble hit us again. And we were a pretty unhappy crew.

Next day came, and I was sick of standing in garages. The mechanic had honestly thought he had found all my troubles but then it became obvious that something was wrong in the differential. He said go on and drive it and I'll look for a used rear end and maybe we can do the job for twenty-five instead of a hundred dollars. It was another bad weather day so I said, "Let's go up to Whiteface Mountain." This was about 120 miles to the NW near Lake Placid and I could take the kids to the North Pole. We went, and the scenery was really out of this world—almost vertical cliffs and great mountains. It was a real thrill for all of us, even though the day was not sunny. All along the way we saw signs for "Ausable Chasm." The Ausable is a vicious river in those parts and we were driving along it part of the way, but we never actually saw the chasm which I hear is quite a sight. Now you'll soon learn that we saw our own sight.

It was on our way back and we were again driving beside the Ausable and beneath the cliffs. I had stopped a couple of times and we'd gotten out of the car and stood in amazement looking up and down at the beauties around us. Farther on, I saw these tremendous rapids in the Ausable and pulled over to the side of the road. We got out. We then walked down toward the rapids and stood on a flat boulder the size of a large house. The noise was deafening and we could barely yell at each other and be heard. Up the river a couple hundred feet it was calm and placid with a glass-like surface—then it began to tumble through and over boulders and gather speed. From a width of probably a hundred feet it was squeezed into a narrow space about eight feet across in the area just below us—and I recall telling myself that no man could last in that raceway, and figured the water must be travelling about thirty miles per hour. It was then that Jean screamed. I turned from gazing down the river and I looked down below us just as the water folded over one of the kids. Jean says I screamed "Bruce!"— but I don't think I did because I jumped in thinking I was going after Chris. There was no decision about whether to jump or not jump. I was in. I did not and do not know how deep it was. I do know the water got deeper.

When I got hold of Bruce the first time, I couldn't see him. I was afraid he had struck his head on a rock and was knocked out. Then I lost him. It was then that the water got deeper and I got him again. There was no sensation of being wet or that the water was cold. I recall now that I was bumping my knees on hard objects and that I was glad to see that the water was more calm ahead if I could push us over out of the main stream and I had no doubt but I would be able to. And then we were climbing out, grappling up a rock. It was then that I realized that Jean had also jumped in right behind me and had never caught up. But she was all right. I remembered that I thought it was good she had jumped in because I can't swim. And it was only at that moment that I had given the slightest thought to that fact. Probably not more than fifteen or twenty seconds after I jumped in, we were all three out, soaked, in a complete state of shock, and terribly frightened.

I then found out that my knees were all cut and bloody from hitting rocks and Jean was hugging Bruce and the kids— the others were huddled into a little knot, some crying, others just stupefied. Bruce had been hypnotized by the movement of the water and had been drawn in. He had felt no fear, no sensation of wet or cold and had not tried to swim, which would have done no good anyway. He was very aware, though, that he had lost his brand new harmonica which we very soon replaced, and very happily.

We rode the hundred miles back to camp in our wet clothes. But this is not entirely a true statement. We didn't get back to camp without more car trouble. It failed us three times on the main street of Ticonderoga and again, I found a fine mechanic, who fixed the trouble. Anyway, we got back to camp, built a big campfire and sat around it. We rehashed our thoughts. And we were quiet and so very thankful and so completely aware that we had not been alone and had had so little to do with saving ourselves. It was at bedtime that Jeff came to Jean who was sitting near the fire and he very quietly said, "We better go to church Sunday." Jean and I sat for a long time alone. I think we began to fully realize that this was the reason we had come on vacation to this place and face this trouble. We had been shown the insignificance of car trouble and job problems and the things which had seemingly grown in their importance. They no longer had the importance of a few hours before. Oh, they were still problems, but they had none of the consequence we had assumed. And probably at that moment, more than any other in our family lifetime, we were given closeness and a reason for being that we have never known before.

I have often thought to myself that I would like to really experience God. So many people have made the claim for themselves—and I have never believed all of them. Yet I have been certain such a thing was possible. I can tell you now that I have and that our family has taken on mellowness and a love and patience that we have never known before.

We did go to church as Jeff said we should. We had no Sunday clothes and couldn't find a Presbyterian Church. But we found a little Baptist church where the people were singing at the top of their voices. We wanted to sit on the back row because of the way we looked and the people were standing, which was fine. But they were on the last stanza and when they sat down there was no back row and we were all standing up and feeling mighty conspicuous. A couple elders got us some folding chairs and we sat through a fine sermon. The minister greeted us from the pulpit, and we had to stand up again, and I had to tell them where we were from and who we were. I wanted to tell them the reason why we were there but I didn't. I felt then and I feel now that this isn't something to talk about—but rather something very personal from which our family will forever benefit. No one else could really understand anything but the horror we knew. They couldn't know the good ending.

Now to finish with the vacation. We started home on a fine day, left at one o'clock in the afternoon, three hundred miles from home. Halfway, the car really let us down. We blew a head gasket, and had water coming out of the tail pipe. A little inquiry, and I knew this was a hundred-dollar job, plus motel. And I didn't have that kind of money. So, what to do? We got off the NY Thruway and started organizing. We filled everything that would hold water. We found that by going five miles at a time, we could stop, take off the radiator cap without it steaming a lot, fill up with two gallons, and go another five miles. This would work, as long as we could replenish our water supply every three stops. There were not a few times when the limit was almost reached without our finding a water source—but we made a hundred and fifty miles in this manner, got home at one-thirty in the morning, and the car hasn't moved since.

This was our vacation. It was dreadful. Yet it was good. We cannot say that we did not have a good time. Yet we would never do it again if we could know that was ahead.

This would be a good time for me to assume that I will never get off my back. I don't feel that way. I feel wonderful. I know why, so do we all, and so do you.

All Our Love,

Wallace

(But, Dad—you forgot the part about your sailor cap still being on your head and your pipe in your mouth. I guess you thought they'd never believe that.)

✠   ✠   ✠

But now, here I was, back in the Poconos, sitting in traffic.

"Mary, what do you think?" Ed asked again, aware that my mind was somewhere else.

"Vacation? Sure, hon, I could use a break."

Jamie and I looked through the travel guide and made some calls. We decided to drive down to the Outer Banks in North Carolina. Ed and I had been to a Carolina beach on our honeymoon and remembered the shore there was quite nice.

Reservations were made at a hotel right on the beach. The vacation was looking better all the time.

"I'll be fine," Flip assured us as we prepared to leave.

"We'll call with a phone number as soon as we get there, Flip." Ed promised.

Gram looked flustered. Ed sat her down and explained to her our plans.

"Have a lovely time, dear," she kept saying as we backed out of the driveway.

Our children had grown since our last vacation, but still displayed their particular traveling traits.

Jamie was a great traveler from the time he was born. When he was seven months old we traveled halfway across the country at Christmas to visit my grandparents in Missouri. The van was cold and drafty—the temperature outside reaching a frigid seventeen below with treacherous road conditions. He kept us amused, smiling and laughing, content the entire trip.

When we ventured out to Indiana, another long haul, Jamie was three and Christopher was added to the picture. Jamie said few words for the entire trip, content to look out the window, taking in the countryside. He was always proud of the fact he never fell asleep in the car on a trip.

Chris was another story. He cried, fussed, whined, and

screamed from the time we left home until our return. I was always searching for ways to distract and entertain him. As he got older we'd play games such as "I'm thinking of an animal." Someone would describe an animal, its color, size, the sound that it made, and someone else would guess what it was. If he was correct, it was then his turn to think of an animal. It kept Chris entertained for a while.

"Remember the game Jamie came up with when he was five?" Ed asked me, obviously amused by the thought. We were then driving well on our way south. How could I forget?

"Wasn't it 'I'm thinking of a disease'"? I replied. We all laughed.

"Yes," Ed said, "but don't you remember when he suggested it? Right after I told you how hungry I was and suggested we stop for something to eat."

Jamie had always loved books. When Jamie was three years old, Ed took him to a mall and stood him between a bookstore and a large toy store.

"Which store do you want to go into, Jamie?" he asked.

"That one!" Jamie replied, pointing to the bookstore.

After looking around, totally engrossed in all the possibilities, he selected a book about great sailing ships, and Ed bought it for him. He spent hours studying its pages, which depicted sailing vessels from around the world. As he grew, his love for books increased, and he became an avid reader. We realized when he was very young that Jamie was an extremely bright, gifted young man.

At four years old, he got hold of a book from our own collection, entitled *The Human Body Book.* It was quite detailed, explaining the various functions of the systems and organs within the human body. He loved it and often studied it. It had pictures of various diseases that could invade the body. They were not actual photographs, yet they still sent a bit of a chill through me when I looked at them.

"Mom, they're just pictures of real diseases," he'd explain to me. So when Jamie suggested playing "I'm thinking of a disease"—he was well prepared. I guess if we had grabbed at the idea, he would have gone into detail, giving us clues, symptoms of the diseases, and so on. The rest of us unanimously decided to come up with another game we would all enjoy and postponed stopping for lunch for a bit.

"I really don't like these long trips," Chris sighed, sinking down into his seat.

"I know, hon, you never have," I added.

"Remember our last vacation," Jamie asked, "when we had two flat tires in ten minutes?"

"Don't remind us," I interrupted. "This one's going to be different. We have all new tires. We even have reservations this time."

We had taken a few days off the previous summer and headed for Washington D.C. Ed thought it would be nice to spend the Fourth of July in our nation's capital. We realized, as we attempted to get a hotel room, that thousands of other people had that very same thought. Ed remembered the hotel he and the boys had stayed in a few years earlier.

"I remember just where it is!" he assured me. We had been driving in heavy rain all day. It was now a downpour so intense that our wipers were of no use. As we pulled up in front of the hotel, we could see the building was now surrounded by a cyclone fence topped with barbed wire—abandoned and permanently closed.

"Well, it really was a nice place," Ed said as we drove away.

We were told we could find a room in Crystal City, right outside Washington, so we headed there. We were all weary from the trip.

"Mary, run in and see if there are any rooms," Ed said stopping alongside the curb in front of a large, fifteen-story hotel. I approached the desk and asked the clerk about available accommodations.

"Yes, I have two rooms, but they are not adjoining."

I was very hesitant about that. We had always either stayed in one room, or had two rooms with a door in between. I ran out to ask Ed.

"We'd better take them," he said. "It's getting late and we may not find another place."

"OK, hon," I said hesitantly.

He helped me unload the suitcases and necessary essentials for the night.

"Jamie and I will go park the car; you get the keys and wait here in the lobby for us."

The lobby was spacious and bustling with activity. David was tired, leaning heavily on my side as I made the necessary arrangements. Dawn and Chris sat with the luggage, taking in all the commotion around them.

Suddenly, an alarm sounded. Everyone looked at one another, startled and confused.

"That's the fire alarm!" the clerk said loudly enough for people to hear and spread the word.

"Please exit the front doors," he instructed us.

"See if you can drag this suitcase out, Chris," I said, grabbing David's hand.

"Where are Dad and Jamie?" Dawn asked with obvious concern.

"They're parking the car. They'll find us, don't worry," I answered.

We headed out the front doors along with dozens of other people, dragging our luggage behind us. We were instructed to stand on the sidewalk as the fire engines pulled up. Firemen leaped off the trucks and filed into the building but after about twenty minutes determined that there was no actual fire. Ed and Jamie were still nowhere to be found.

The fire engines pulled away and people dispersed as the children and I stood alone, waiting for Ed. Finally they returned.

"Where have you been?" I asked, obviously worried.

"We have been stuck in the parking garage all this time. The elevators wouldn't work. It's a good thing there wasn't really a fire!" he said.

That was it! We made a decision. Ed went to the clerk at the desk.

"There's no way we can keep those two separate rooms after all that commotion. We can't be separated from our children. Could we please have our money back?" he asked.

"I have a better idea," the clerk said, understanding our concern.

"I have a luxury suite on the tenth floor that will fit all of you nicely. I'll give it to you for half price." We agreed, and it turned out he was right—the suite was luxurious. We got a good night's sleep and awoke to a beautiful morning, slightly overcast, but not threatening. We were ready for a day of sightseeing. The children were anxious.

"Mommy, can we wait out in the hall?" Dawn asked eagerly.

"OK, just stay together; we're almost ready."

Within a minute or two, Chris returned to the door.

"Mom, you won't believe this! David pushed the button for the elevator. He got on it and went down!"

Realizing this was a fifteen-floor hotel, and David, only three, could exit on any of those floors and take a walk, I was frightened. Of course, visions of lurking child abductors took first place in my mind—certainly a very real concern in our world today. I took the adjoining elevator to the lobby to report him as missing, just in case we didn't find him immediately. When I returned to our floor and exited the elevator, David was stepping off the one he had taken at the same time.

"David! There you are!" I said as I grabbed him to hug him. "How did you know which floor to get off on?"

"I saw Daddy push the button on top," he said, quite proud of himself. "It's the number ten!"

We reminded everyone of the importance of staying together at all times and were on our way.

We took the subway from Crystal City to Washington D.C. and boarded an escalator that took us to the street above. As we moved steadily upward, surrounded by other equally anxious tourists, Ed and I looked over at the "down" escalator, crowded with drenched, vinyl-clad tourists clutching umbrellas—obviously relieved to be inside. Ed and I looked at one another realizing there was no turning back. We stepped out into a soaking downpour. Soon, however, the sun broke through the clouds and the rain stopped.

That evening we attended a fireworks display overlooking the White House lawn. The fireworks were spectacular! Not nearly as breathtaking, however, was the thought that all the hundreds of people seated around us would also be heading for the subway at midnight.

It was a mad rush, but we made it.

✠   ✠   ✠

But this vacation would surely be different; none of that wondering if we'd find a place to stay. Our rooms were awaiting our arrival. That was a comforting thought.

Upon entering the Outer Banks, I noticed a sign posted outside the visitors' center as we pulled up to it. It was a warning to swimmers of possible dangerous undertow due to the recent turbulent weather.

We arrived at the hotel and unloaded the car. The hotel proved a good choice—it was situated right on the beach and had a swimming pool. Dawn and David were still a bit frightened of the ocean.

Our room was clean and nice. Dawn ran directly to the balcony overlooking the ocean.

"Can we go collect shells now, Mommy?" she asked anxiously.

"Let's get our bags unpacked first, hon, and then we'll go to the beach," I answered.

"Jamie's already at the beach," Chris informed me. "Can't I go swimming too?"

I dropped my bag on the bed and made my way over to the balcony. There was no one on the beach. The sky was overcast, and the water appeared to be quite choppy. Sure enough, I could see Jamie running toward the water with his boogie board under one arm.

Maybe there's a reason no one else is in the water, I thought in a panic. "Ed, let's go to the beach," I said, rushing out the door.

As the little ones trailed behind me, grabbing my hands, I had the distinct feeling I had come this way before.

We reached the shoreline in time to see Jamie on his stomach, paddling towards the shore, but making little progress. He was quite a ways out.

"Jamie, come in here!" Ed yelled.

"I'm trying!" he yelled back.

He continued paddling furiously, but was not getting any closer to the shore. In fact, he appeared to be drifting farther and farther out.

Oh, Lord, I prayed. *Please, bring my son back safely!*

There were no lifeguards; we were the only ones on the beach.

"Jamie, paddle sideways—like this!"

Ed walked along the shore, demonstrating and moving his arms. Jamie managed to turn the board sideways, and ride the waves running nearly parallel to the shore. Very slowly the current brought him to shore. He was noticeably shaken.

"No one comes to the beach alone or without permission, do you all understand?" Ed warned.

As we walked back toward the hotel, I breathed a sigh of relief and thought, *I'm beginning to feel like I'm on vacation.*

The next few days were surprisingly relaxing. In fact, I almost forgot for a time that we were on vacation. The sun was high in the clear southern sky, the sand clean and white. Dawn collected shells to her heart's content. The sun's rays shining through the waves lent a translucent, aqua cast to the water—irresistible to Ed and the boys, who loved swimming in the ocean. I was back and forth between pool and shore, taking David and Dawn for swims. When on the beach, David spent his time wrapped in a hooded, terry cloth jacket, in an attempt to protect that fair, redheaded skin.

"Mom, wait until you see the guys rappelling off the hotel!" Jamie said with great anticipation, the day before we were to leave for home.

"What? You're kidding," I replied.

"No, come and see! You won't believe it!"

We walked toward the side of the building, and sure enough—

on the very top, six floors up, three young men, possibly in their mid-twenties, were preparing to do . . . I wasn't sure exactly what.

"Wait until you see this, Mom. It's called Australian rappelling," Jamie explained.

Right before my eyes, one of the young men grabbed a rope (hopefully attached to something), and proceeded to run down the side of the building, headfirst.

I'm happy to say he made it safely to the ground.

"I don't believe it," I said, shaking my head.

"He learned that in the army. Isn't that cool?"

"How do you know so much, Jamie?" I asked, concerned that he was a little too intrigued.

"I was talking to them before. They were swimming at the pool and told me about it."

Later that day, as I was leaving the room to do a small load of laundry, I noticed Chris and Dawn at an open window at the end of the hall. They were straining their necks to look up. They seemed to be half-laughing and half-scared.

"Are they at it again?" I called to them.

"Mom, you better see this!" Chris said with a look I did not like at all.

I ran to the window, stuck my head out, and looked up in time to see Jamie on top of the building with the others. He was securing the harness around his waist as I had seen the young man do before his headfirst descent.

"OH, NO YOU DON'T, JAMIE! YOU COME DOWN HERE IMMEDIATELY," I yelled.

He slipped out of the harness and came down immediately.

"What do you think you are doing? Do you want this to be your last day on earth?" I asked.

"Oh, Mom, I was up taking pictures for them, and one of them said I could try it. The other one said I couldn't, because his insurance wouldn't cover me. So, don't worry, I couldn't have tried it anyway."

The car was packed up. We pulled onto the highway and headed north.

When we arrived home, Gram was outside waiting for us, pacing back and forth in the carport.

"I was so worried!" she said as she hugged us.

"Oh, Edward, she was up here constantly looking for you and the family," said Flip.

"I'm sorry, Flip," he said as he hugged her.

"You know," he continued, looking at me, "I guess we've taken our last vacation for a while. We just can't leave Gram," he concluded.

"No more vacations for a while," I mused, and I breathed a sigh of relief.

GRANDMA ON DUTY 6

"Now, don't stand on ceremony. Make yourself right at home!" Gram would admonish her guests.

When Gram was healthy, one of her admirable graces was her ability to make people feel welcome. And she did. She took great care to see that everyone was comfortable, had enough to eat, sat in the right chair, and had the proper clothing.

"Have a piece of pie, darling—I just made it today."

"You look cold, darling—let me get you a sweater."

As the disease progressed it became increasingly difficult to spend time with her, because she would go to extraordinary measures to make everyone around her "comfortable." If one of the boys was relaxing on the floor she would offer him a pillow. If they declined her offer she would then insist he needed a pillow in order to really be comfortable. They learned to simply take the pillow rather than listen to her further instructions. She would go around the room and instruct each person how they could be most comfortable.

"Mary, sit over by your husband."

"Edward, make room for your wife."

A few seconds later she would address the next person.

"Margaretta, move your chair over here."

"David, tie your shoe and tuck your shirt into your pants.

Mary, make him tuck his shirt in." If she did not get an immediate response she would repeat the instruction more emphatically.

"Christopher, you're a handsome young man. You'd be much more handsome if you would drop a few pounds. Get down on the floor and do some sit-ups. I do fifty every morning, you know. You should too!"

She would pass the candy dish around the room. By the third time around, someone would usually get annoyed and hide it.

"Edward, are you finished with your coffee yet?"

"No, Gram, it's too hot to drink."

"Mary, are you finished with your coffee?"

"Not yet, Grandma."

A few minutes later she would again ask about our progress. Halfway finished, and the cup was swept up, washed, dried, and put away almost before you could reach for it again. It was rare to see a dirty dish in her sink.

In her never ending desire to be helpful, Gram would come upstairs and make sure all my dishes were washed. This became a source of great frustration for me. There were mornings I would leave to take the children to school and return home to find all the breakfast dishes had been washed and put away.

Now, really, what busy mother wouldn't welcome such a surprise?

The problem was that Gram had decided that the use of soap was "unnecessary, darling." Needless to say, I had to search and rewash. As the months progressed I would see her take a dirty dish, dry it, and put it away. She skipped the wash cycle altogether! No matter what I would say, how nicely I would approach her, she was determined to do my dishes. She would not stop until every dish was put away, and the dishtowel was draped neatly over the sink. This became my signal. If I returned home and spied the towel draped neatly over the sink, I knew I was in trouble.

One morning, as I rushed to leave, I couldn't help but cringe as I placed the dishes in the kitchen.

"That was a great omelet, Mom!" Jamie said, placing his dish on the stack.

A cheese omelet—I could not face the possibility of Gram washing these dishes. I reached under the sink and shut off the water.

Why hadn't I thought of that before? The perfect solution! I backed out of the driveway, confident I had—at last—solved the problem.

I returned home to find the dishtowel draped neatly over the sink. Had she discovered my secret? I pulled a dish from the cupboard, and it was obvious she had not.

"Grandma, you washed my dishes?"

"Why yes, darling," she answered looking up from her knitting.

"Grandma, how could you wash the dishes without any water?"

"Oh, but darling—there was a little drip."

I returned upstairs on the verge of tears. I realized I was losing control of my home. It was obvious that whatever Gram determined to do she was going to find a way to do it. That was a most unsettling thought.

Her doctor prescribed medications to help control her agitation. There seemed to be little change. We were dealing not only with a disease, but with a person of iron will, as well.

Gram possessed absolute resolve and accomplished whatever she
made up her mind to do. I think back over the years and marvel
over the times I stood in disbelief at something she had "taken on"
and, through her resolve, accomplished. I recall a juniper bush
that had become so overgrown it resembled a tree, crowding her
view from the kitchen window.

"It must come down, Margaretta!" she announced one morning as she finished her coffee.

Later that day I drove up to see her standing where that juniper had been the day before. She was out of breath, her face red
and glistening with perspiration, brushing the dirt from her
knees. Even the massive root had been excavated from the earth.

This resolve quickly became a force in our home; a force that
could hardly be controlled. It led to numerous accidents and
emergency room visits.

One afternoon as I was taking dinner out of the oven,
Grandma decided she would carry an open coffee can filled with
turpentine into the kitchen. She had been out on the deck and had
discovered it on the table where a painting project was in process.

I cautioned her at once, "Please leave it there, Gram."

She continued toward the kitchen. The oven was hot, the door
wide open. The pan I was removing was heavy, containing a sizzling

roast complete with potatoes and drippings. I feared she would not listen to me.

"Please wait, Grandma!"

On she came. Her knees hit the oven door and buckled. The spring broke, forcing her shoulder into the oven. Her glasses shattered, and the turpentine—combined with the greasy drippings—flew everywhere, covering cabinets and the kitchen floor.

I thanked the Lord—out loud—that it had not ignited near the open flame.

I lifted her off the oven door and checked her for burns. She appeared to be fine.

"Let's get you to the living room so you can sit while I clean up in here." The floor was a slippery mess.

Within moments she was on her feet again.

"I must go downstairs and get my glasses."

"Grandma, your glasses broke when you fell into the oven. Don't you remember?"

"When did I fall? That's ridiculous! They must be downstairs. I'll go ask Margaretta." Off she went.

The stairs were also quickly becoming a problem. There was no door separating the main house from the apartment, so any uneasy thought or concern would bring Grandma up to relieve her mind.

"Where is Margaretta?" she would often ask.

"She's downstairs, Grandma."

"She is not down there. She must be outside."

She would go to the doors and windows searching in vain for her sister. I would sometimes send or escort her down to look again. There came a day, however, when she no longer recognized her sister at all.

"Where is Margaretta?" she asked, looking directly at her sister.

"I am Margaretta, Laura."

"You are not Margaretta."

She became quite indignant. There was no convincing her. We finally had Flip put on her coat, go outside, and come in the door as if she had been somewhere.

"Here is Margaretta!" we assured her.

It worked.

Gram put her arms around her sister and hugged her.

"Oh, Sister, where have you been?" she asked, obviously relieved.

It was a chilling moment. Big changes were taking place daily now.

✢   ✢   ✢

It was not long before conventional days and nights were gone from our household. One morning I was awakened at around one o'clock in the morning by the peculiar sound of the coffeemaker downstairs brewing a fresh pot of coffee. I made my way halfway down the stairs and saw freshly cut grapefruit served on two place settings. The toast was almost ready to pop up; there was bacon sizzling in the pan.

"Good morning, darling!" Gram greeted me heartily.

"Grandma, I think maybe you set your alarm to the wrong time. It's only one o'clock in the morning."

We both laughed a bit and went back to bed.

It was not as easy to convince her on other nights. She would be sound asleep at nine o'clock and would emerge an hour later from her bedroom fully dressed for the new day—often in a suit with stockings and high heels.

"Gram, it's nighttime. Go back to bed," Jamie would tell her.

"Good morning, Jamie," she would reply.

He would open the drapes to reveal the blackness of the night.

"Look out there, Gram. It's ten o'clock at night."

"Laura, Jamie's right, let's go to bed," Flip would say.

"Oh, you're all crazy!" Gram would conclude.

I was concerned that Gram might use the stove during the night and start a fire. I became alert for any unusual sounds. One night I heard a rustling sound in the living room at two o'clock in the morning. I hadn't heard any footsteps on the stairs. Could it be Grandma? I was startled at the sight of a mouse-like creature scurrying into a corner. (Actually, I think it was more startled by my ensuing shrill scream.) Ed followed the scream and appeared close behind. He was thrilled.

"You scared him, hon! Isn't he beautiful?"

"What is it?" I asked, ready to jump up onto the couch.

"It's a flying squirrel!"

I had to admit he was pretty cute. His beautiful, big eyes looked frightened, but I knew I would not sleep unless he was outside. Ed returned him to the outdoors, and we went back to bed.

The night, however, was young. Jamie had a visitor at three o'clock that morning. He had taken a piece of pie to bed and left a portion of it on the table beside him.

"Jamie, darling, sit up and finish your pie. It's very good!"

Even in the middle of the night, Gram thought it her duty to see that everyone was well taken care of.

Jamie got up and escorted her back to her room. We were all learning to expect the unexpected—night and day.

The following evening, the flying squirrel found its way back into the house. This time Ed woke Dawn up to see it.

"Daddy, I told my science teacher about the flying squirrel, and he said they make good pets. Can't we keep him?"

"Well, not for long. Maybe for a day or so."

Dawn disappeared and moments later returned with a cage recently vacated by a very naughty gerbil. I had been convinced that the gerbil would be a harmless, trouble-free pet. He escaped, and weeks later I discovered him living in the sofa. The children were concerned he might have starved to death. He had managed to find plenty to eat, though, namely the entire underside of the sofa cushions.

"Now, Dawn, remember, we have cats, and they will be very interested in getting ahold of this little guy. He's not about to go to sleep."

"I know, Daddy, they're nocturnal. They stay up all night."

"Well, he's come to the right house. Let's go back to bed."

✝ ✝ ✝

The cats were not the only ones intrigued by our latest houseguest. Ed brought the cage downstairs to show him to Gram and Flip and placed it on the table.

"My, isn't he lovely, Edward?" Gram said as she looked into the cage.

Ed asked Flip for a knitting needle so he could point out the flaps of skin that enabled him to fly.

"Are you going to pierce him, Edward?"

"Of course not, Gram," Ed assured her. We looked at one another, startled by her question. "We'll keep him until tomorrow, and then I think we'd better let him go."

The following morning we left to do some shopping. While we were out, Gram made a trip upstairs and discovered the cat playing with the cage—very interested in the squirrel. Flip came up to look for Gram in time to see the cat pull the cage to the ground. The squirrel escaped and darted under the table. Gram got between them and attempted to pick up the squirrel.

"Leave him alone, Laura! He might bite you!"

She got down on her knees and cornered him. She pulled the cage across the floor, determined to get the squirrel back inside.

"Laura, stop!"

The squirrel crawled up her arm, gnawing and tearing as he clawed his way to her elbow. We walked in just in time to get her to the emergency room. Our main concern was rabies.

"How did this happen?" the emergency room doctor asked.

Gram did not have any idea. She just smiled at him and said, "My, but aren't you a good-looking young man!"

I smiled and then attempted to explain what had happened.

"What about rabies?" I asked anxiously.

"Believe it or not, squirrels rarely carry rabies. In fact, we have never had a case of rabies reported having been transmitted by a squirrel, so relax."

He cleaned up the bites, and we returned home.

The squirrel was gone, never to return—at least if he knew what was good for him.

SHOPPING  8

"*M*argaretta and I are going to dash up to Hess's Department Store in Allentown," Gram would often tell me.

Gram loved shopping and had boundless energy. She had a flair for fashion, and when fully dressed in her latest purchase, was most elegant.

Before she became sick, whenever Ed and I would go out for an evening and drop the children off for the night, she would lead me into her bedroom and over to her full-length mirror.

"I have just the thing for your outfit, darling!" she would assure me.

She'd pull a four-inch wide leather belt with a large enamel or brass buckle on it out of her dresser and fasten it around my waist as she looked into the mirror.

"What do you think?" she'd say admiringly.

Five-foot-two-inches, divided by four, I looked like a short, little weight lifter—or maybe a stunted gladiator.

"Gram, it would look great on you, but it's just not me."

"How about this, dear . . ." she'd continue, reaching into her closet to remove a natty-looking blazer from its hanger. "This would look lovely on you."

I'd try it on and occasionally be convinced to perk up my

attire, but most often I'd leave the room in my familiar, comfortable clothes.

Then there were those special moments when she would reach deep into the wooden bench that sat beneath her bedroom window.

"I just finished this yesterday, darling. Try it on!"

I'd slip into a knitted jacket or sweater of lusciously soft wool, a one-of-a-kind creation, and I'd have to smile.

"It's beautiful, Gram!"

"It looks lovely on you, dear. It's yours," she'd say with a smile.

We'd hug, and she'd pat me.

"Now, you and your husband go out and have a beautiful evening!" she'd insist. "And don't worry about the children."

This was a blessing to a young couple, to have someone to keep your children for an evening, and realize they were in good hands. At that time we were confident she could handle whatever might come up.

She loved to dress Ed up as well, although he often wouldn't stand for it. On his birthday she'd often present him with a magnificent, hand-knit sweater, of an intricate pattern that only a skilled perfectionist as herself could create. The sweaters were so exquisite that heads would turn when he wore them. People often commented on their unique beauty.

There was a special Christmas gift she presented to Ed when he was eighteen. He unwrapped the large package and pulled out a white, three-quarter-length canvas coat with a plush white lamb's-wool lining and collar. It was gorgeous! He and I were both trying to picture him hopping on his motorcycle and taking off on one wheel, as was his custom, wearing this coat.

But that was Gram.

"Why don't you come along with us, dear? We're going shopping," she'd coax. Most of the time I would decline. I was simply too busy with the children, although they were always invited as well. On the few occasions I did go along, I could see that she was truly "in her element."

✠   ✠   ✠

Gram was extremely outgoing, ready with a hearty greeting for everyone she met, a loving smile, or gentle pat on the head of a child. She was always free with compliments.

"That's a lovely sweater you have on."

"My, what a beautiful baby!"

Everyone she passed felt a little better about his or her day. She especially enjoyed when her great-grandchildren came along.

"These are my great-grandchildren," she would announce.

"You don't look old enough to be a great-grandmother!"

"Well, I am!" she would reply.

She would smile and often quote a verse from Proverbs 17:6, "Grandchildren are the crown of the aged" (NRSV).

"And they certainly are!" she would add.

Because shopping and working in department stores had been such a pleasant part of her life, I wanted to take her shopping as long as possible after we moved.

As the disease progressed, she was still outgoing and verbal to people she encountered, but her comments were those that previously would have remained unspoken. She was becoming like a child—painfully candid.

Walking across the parking lot one afternoon, headed for the grocery store to do our shopping, we passed a woman enjoying an ice-cream cone.

"No wonder she's so fat, eating all that ice cream!"

It was obvious we were in for quite an interesting shopping trip.

We made it through several aisles without incident. Stopping at the meat department, I stood looking over the packaged chicken. I noticed Grandma handling a roast that had been coated with parsley and various other spices. She had a troubled expression on her face. The gentleman next to her was busy comparing prices.

"Imagine . . . selling meat covered with bugs!" she said, looking in his direction.

The gentleman, obviously taken aback by her comment, smiled and walked away.

And we were not even halfway through the store.

I learned to distract and steer her away from overweight people, or anyone dressed in an unusual manner—skirt too short, hair too long.

I'm sure the woman waiting in line in front of us was shocked when Gram tucked her bra strap inside her shirt for her. At times I would try to explain. Other times I would look the other way, wishing I could fall through the floor. We finally reached the checkout.

She studied the girl at the register.

"Look at her hairdo. Isn't that ridiculous!"

"That will be $69.72," announced the embarrassed checkout girl.

To her amazement and my shock, Grandma opened her pocketbook and removed a stack of bills—$1,500 to be exact. I watched her slowly count out the money. Somehow she was still able to do so. Flip and I looked at one another with the same realization: Grandma would soon not be responsible enough to handle money. She must have sensed our concern. Over the next few weeks, she hid her pocketbook several times a day so that even she did not know where it was. Sometimes it was under the mattress, in a drawer, in a cupboard. Flip could not rest until it was found— again and again.

As the months passed I would take her out in public only when I had no choice. One afternoon, Flip had a doctor's appointment, and there was no one to stay with Grandma, so I brought her along. We entered the waiting room, and I'm sure I breathed a sigh of relief when I looked around and realized we were the only ones waiting.

"Come and sit down, Grandma."

After a period of about thirty seconds, she began.

"When is Margaretta coming out? She's been gone a long time."

"No, Gram, it's only been a short time. Let's be patient."

Within a few minutes the door opened, and much to my

horror, a very large woman entered. I grabbed a magazine and tried to distract Grandma, making it somewhat of a shield.

"My, Mary," she said as she pushed the magazine aside. "Did you ever in your life see such a fat woman?"

It was loud and clear and irretrievable.

"Here is a magazine. Please read it," I said, looking her straight in the eyes.

She flipped through the pages and paused as if she had found something that interested her.

"Don't we know this woman?"

"Yes, Gram, that's Audrey Hepburn. You've seen her in movies."

By this time, the waiting room was filling with other patients. She continued turning pages. Maybe we would get out of there without further incident.

"Listen to this, darling," she said, clearing her throat so she could read more clearly. "Is your husband meeting all your sexual expectations?"

The ground refused to swallow me up. It was one of those awful moments when your only wish is to become invisible. I could not look up. I sank deep into the chair.

"Let's turn the page, Gram. Look at this adorable baby."

Minutes dragged on.

"Let's go for a walk outside," I suggested.

As I escorted her to the door I noticed some people staring. One nodded reassuringly as if maybe she understood. As soon as we were out the door, Gram grabbed my arm and wanted me to dance across the parking lot with her.

"All around the mulberry bush, the monkey chased the weasel," she sang.

I'm sure it was a sight to behold. At first I felt terribly embarrassed, but then I was stricken with the realization of who this woman was—this oh-so-lovely, elegant, proud woman—and my heart went out to her. I held her arm a bit tighter and we skipped to the car.

Our "outings" ended one afternoon when she began searching for Flip while we were traveling home.

"Where is Margaretta?" she asked.

"She is sitting next to you, Gram," I assured her as I looked into my rearview mirror.

"We left her there. Go back!" she said frantically.

"I'm right here, Laura," Flip assured her.

"Go back, now! How could you leave her there?"

She was angry.

She reached for the door handle and tried to get it open. Flip grabbed her. I quickly pulled off the road.

"Gram, do not open the door. Flip is right here." I assured her.

She could not be convinced. Flip restrained her for the last few miles.

At times, after these situations were over and I was able to put my own frustration aside, I would think about the emotions Grandma must have been experiencing. I think the horror of a loved one missing—especially your child—would top anyone's list of dreaded emotions. To experience these feelings, as Gram did, and yet have no one believe you must have been dreadful.

We could only watch as Grandma's perception of reality grew increasingly distorted. We would notice her smiling and waving at the newsmen on television.

"Gram, what are you doing?" one of the children would ask.

"He waved to me, so I waved back to him."

"Gram, you can see him, but he can't see you. He's on television."

But she was so convinced that she would no longer eat her dinner in front of the TV. She thought it was rude.

The same distortion was true of magazines. Gram held up a magazine with a picture of Arnold Schwartzenegger on the front cover.

"My, but aren't you a good-looking young man!" she said with a broad grin, as if no one else was in the room but Arnold and her.

Jamie didn't say anything, he just shook his head and smiled. He was learning, as we all were, that explanations really meant nothing. Often these misconceptions were harmless, but as her condition worsened, they stopped being only fleeting thoughts.

Grandma seemed to get an idea stuck in her mind for weeks, sometimes longer. It would remain an unresolved problem for her and an endurance test for the rest of us. One month she was looking for the hair product that made hair grow overnight. Her hair had become thin, and she claimed she had once purchased such a product in a little black bottle. At first we tried reasoning with her.

"Gram, it is impossible for hair to grow overnight."

That approach was useless. She would make a trip upstairs every ten minutes or so to ask about this product and where she could buy it. This literally went on for weeks. I assured her I had looked in every drugstore in the area. Actually, I had, hoping to find a shampoo that made such a ridiculous claim.

I didn't want to buy something and tell her it would do the trick, though I'd been told this was a good way to handle such a situation. In fact, I often struggled with my Christian belief that I should be honest in my speech to everyone. Should I, due to her condition, set that aside and tell her things that are untrue to console her? She asked anyone and everyone she could find. She even asked the nice gentleman in the garden center.

"Which aisle would have the hair product to make your hair grow overnight?"

This constant, absurd repetition came close to driving me crazy. There were days that I had to leave, though I realized that when I returned Gram would be right back upstairs with the same insistent questioning.

One Saturday, I felt I could not take another day hearing about this miracle product. Ed arrived home and, realizing my extreme frustration, took me aside. Gram was heading back upstairs. She had been talking about it for ten minutes.

"What's wrong, hon?"

"I have heard about this hair product until I feel the urge to pull out my own. I just have to get away for a while. Please take over."

"Edward, could you take me to a store to buy this special product? It's in a little black bottle and it makes your hair grow overnight."

"Gram, we have looked everywhere. There is no such product."

"Maybe Bamberger's would have it," she suggested.

"OK—that's it," he announced, "we're going to Bam's!" The mall was at least forty minutes away, but he hoped she would finally give up on this idea if he could settle it, once and for all, in her mind.

It was a ninety-eight-degree summer day and there was no air conditioning in his car. All the windows were down, but it was hot.

"Shut the windows, Edward. You're blowing me away!"

"That's where I draw the line, Gram," he said. "It's ninety-eight degrees! The fresh air is good for us."

Of course that conversation was repeated another half dozen times. As he escorted her into the store, she stopped and looked up at him a bit puzzled.

"Oh, what are we doing here, Edward?"

He forgot his own frustration as he looked at her—he simply hugged her as he so often did.

"Oh, Gram, you are so troubled, aren't you?"

Often that had become the only solution. Reasoning was a thing of the past. Love and reassurance were the only solutions.

$\mathcal{T}$he room was dark, the house uncommonly still. It was four o'clock in the morning. I looked over at Ed, who slept peacefully beside me. The alarm would not go off for another hour, yet I was restless. It was Sunday morning.

DO NOT BE ANXIOUS ABOUT ANYTHING . . .   PHILIPPIANS 4:6, NIV

I prayed that I could apply that scripture to the day ahead. Before very long, I knew I would hear Gram's footsteps on the stairs, her first of many trips upstairs before we would leave for church. I lay quietly, thinking back to when the children were very young—another time when I had struggled with Sunday morning anxiety.

I had always looked forward to Sundays and spending time together as a family. Yet as each child was born, getting everyone fed, dressed, and ready to leave in time for Sunday school was no small feat. Ed left for his office at five to prepare to teach his adult Sunday school class—a highlight of his week.

"It's going to be a great lesson today!" he'd tell me with enviable exuberance. He would summarize his lesson for me as I grabbed last-minute bottles, diapers, and other essentials.

"Is everyone ready? Let's not be late!"

We were rarely late, but I would be so frazzled by the time I sat down in class, I once jokingly confided to an equally frazzled young mother that I often felt I had lost my salvation on the way to church. She nodded in agreement. There always seemed to be a snag, an irresistible mud puddle on the way to the car or a lost shoe—not just lost, but gone forever.

"Mom, Barney dropped my sneaker in the pond!"

"Oh, Jamie, not your only pair of shoes."

✢   ✢   ✢

Barney was our beagle, named affectionately after a dog in Jamie's favorite naptime book, *Barney Beagle Plays Baseball.* We had read that book together so many times that Jamie could recite the whole story to me word for word. We were brainwashed into believing that this breed would make a great companion for a growing boy. This particular dog had failed to meet our high expectations. Although we brought him home as a puppy and diligently trained him—exhausting all the tricks in the book—we could not house-break that dog. He was not especially good with children and was a downright nuisance to the horses on the farm.

Barney would tear out the back door, race up the dirt road behind the house, squeeze under the bottom rail of the corral fence, and begin his chase. He'd single out an unsuspecting horse and chase it until he found the opportunity to latch on to its tail. He'd go for a short, brutal ride as the tormented animal whipped its tail from side to side to rid itself of this badgering pest. On several occasions he was given a swift kick—propelling him a good thirty feet to what we assumed to be his death. We would carry the dazed darling down the hill and place him in the shade of the old apple tree. There, the children would perform a vigil, hoping he would regain consciousness.

"He's alive, Mom!" they would announce, greatly relieved. I have to admit that I had mixed emotions when I heard those words.

Even swimming did not come naturally to the dog. One lazy summer afternoon as the children sat fishing off the dock behind the house, I noticed large bubbles rising to the surface of the murky water. I vaguely made out the motionless image of Barney lying flat on his back at the bottom of the pond. I jumped in and pulled him out of the water, holding him up over my shoulder to help drain his waterlogged body.

"Haven't you ever heard of the doggy paddle?" the children taunted the scared, shivering hound.

Barney enjoyed dropping shoes of any description into the pond—sandals, sneakers, hiking boots—and watching them sink slowly to the bottom. Mammoth snapping turtles were a definite deterrent to my retrieving them.

I suppose it was his keen hunting instinct that caused his restlessness. He was always hot on one trail or another. He would run so fast at times that his legs appeared as a blur beneath him.

One still summer evening we heard Barney's shrill howling through the front door. We called him several times, but he would not be dissuaded. He was seated on his haunches, howling doggedly at something up the tree. There was no way we, or the neighbors for that matter, would be getting to sleep anytime soon. Ed ran out to see what he had treed and determined it to be a raccoon, trembling and frothing at the mouth, most likely a rabid one.

"Mary, get my gun!" he yelled toward the house.

Jamie, still awake and observing the scene from his upstairs bedroom window, blurted out curiously, "Hey, Dad, which one are you going to shoot?"

The tension of the moment was eased. Ed and I looked at each other and laughed.

The sad fact is, though, my son was dead serious.

One afternoon the dog attempted to outrun a delivery truck. He met his match and lay pitifully flat in the middle of Schooley's Mountain Road.

"Well, we have a choice," Ed explained after speaking with the vet. "We can have Barney put to sleep, or the vet will do all he can to save him. Of course, that will cost a lot of money."

He saw all the tearful faces surrounding the dinner table. Even

I persuaded Ed to spend more than our meager budget would allow to save our flattened pet's life.

The first few weeks after the accident he was cared for as an invalid—spending his days in a playpen, fed lovingly in my lap, escorted and assisted to the great outdoors (something quite novel to him). Months later, somewhat recovered, he was back in the saddle again.

Yet, the day we brought David home from the hospital, wrapped tenderly within a blanket, Barney took one look at him and was gone. Perhaps it was the gripping realization that we had brought a second redheaded boy into the house, and he feared he was in for it. We ran an ad, hoping that if someone had taken him into their home they would return him—quite sure they would be anxious to do so. We did not see him again until years later.

"Mary, I think I saw Barney walking down the road tonight," Ed told me one evening as he walked in the house.

"You're kidding! What makes you think it was Barney?" I asked.

"Well, for one thing, he was walking sideways."

Since his accident, Barney had been "out of alignment," and his hind legs did not follow the same path as his front legs.

"It was him," he went on, "I'm almost positive! I stopped the car, called his name, and tried to get him in. He looked right at me and ran the other way."

"Now I'm convinced. That does definitely sound like him," I agreed.

✠   ✠   ✠

"Laura, stay down here!"

Flip's voice could be heard trailing close behind Gram on the stairs. I could tell by the sound of her footsteps that she had heels on and was ready for church. It was only five o'clock.

"I'm going to help the children get ready for church, Margaretta."

"Oh, Laura!"

Up she came to our door, turned the handle, and walked in.

"Mary, I've come to help you make the bed."

"Gram, we're still in our bed," Ed explained. "Please go back downstairs."

"Oh, I'll just see if there's something I can do in the kitchen."

"La-de-da," she began to sing, "Away in a man-ger, no crib for a bed . . . the little Lord Jesus . . ."

Sinking deep into my pillow, I prayed, "Lord, please give me grace to get through this morning."

Ed quickly dressed and left for his office to finish preparing for his class. For a fleeting moment I was tempted to covet his gift of teaching. On the way through the kitchen, he spoke to Gram, "Let's go downstairs with Flip."

"OK, Edward." She grabbed his arm, and he escorted her down the stairs before leaving.

Edward did have a way with his grandmother. It was a source of envy for Flip and I. We would try to convince her to do some-thing—wearing ourselves out reasoning with her—and she would need only see Ed or hear his name to be won over. She thought Ed was her husband, and this became more evident as her condition worsened. The only problem I had with this new development was that I became "the other woman."

I pulled myself out of bed and took a quick shower. Wrapping myself quickly in a towel, I returned to find her making my bed.

"Where are the children?" she asked as she fluffed the pillows with great purpose.

"It's early, Gram. They're all asleep."

"Shall I go wake them?" she asked.

"No, they'll be up soon. Let them sleep a little longer."

She was fully dressed in a suit, stockings, and heels. Her navy blue shoes were a size too small, but she insisted on wearing them even though her feet killed her throughout the day. Her earrings were often upside down, which I would point out to her and help her correct.

Then she went downstairs to change into a completely differ-ent outfit.

"Laura, will you stop changing your clothes? You can't wear that!" Flip said wearily.

Up she came, dressed in a wrinkled suit that appeared as if it had been stuffed in a paper bag. We soon discovered that many of her clothes were stuffed into bags for a future trip.

"Mary, I shudder to think how Gram would feel if she could see herself," Flip said with a sigh.

"Is it time to go, darling?" she'd ask.

"No, Gram, we don't leave until nine o'clock. It's only seven-thirty."

"OK, I'll go tell Margaretta."

I kept track of her trips up and down. She averaged a trip about every five minutes. We had four hours between her first trip up at five o'clock, and when we left at nine. Just doing the math made me tired.

I'm sure that getting ready to go agitated her, but Gram had rarely missed church in fifteen years. We wanted to take her with us as long as possible.

I would hear Flip, downstairs, terribly frustrated with her changing for the fourth and fifth times, and go down to see if I could help.

As we sat talking in her bedroom, Flip showed me the various outfits Gram had tried on and discarded. Before long I heard Ed yelling from our bathroom upstairs.

"Mary, help! Come get Gram!"

I ran upstairs into the steam filled bathroom to find Gram peering through the fogged shower door.

"My, don't you look nice, Edward."

"Mary, take her downstairs!"

"Gram, come out here. Let's go downstairs," I coaxed. She did so—quite reluctantly.

By the time we actually left for church, I was worn and weary. She was still raring to go.

"Come, Margaretta!" she would say as she headed upstairs.

"Oh, Laura, I'm coming," Flip answered, feeling equally worn out.

We piled into our station wagon—designed to seat eight comfortably. Let's just say it seated the eight of us. We were traveling to a church we had attended for ten years before having moved. The ride was thirty minutes.

"David, come and sit up here on my lap," she would begin as we backed out of the driveway.

"Gram, David has to sit in his seat with a seat belt on," I explained.

One minute later . . .

"David, come and sit up here on my lap."

Ed would explain once again that David had to stay in his seat.

One minute later—the same thing. After the fourth or fifth time, the tension would begin to build amidst the eight passengers.

"My, Edward, the trucks are getting bigger all the time!" she would say as a tractor trailer lumbered by.

"Actually, Gram, they're the same size they've always been," Ed pointed out. How sad that her world was becoming so distorted.

"Really, darling? I believe they're bigger," she concluded.

We'd pass through the Delaware Water Gap and each time she'd point out the housing development up on the mountain. In reality, there were no houses for miles around.

"My, look at all the houses up there!" she would say. I would have preferred to just let her comment go, but I was only one of the eight passengers in the car, and someone always corrected her. She would become more emphatic.

"There are most definitely houses on that mountain!"

"All around the mulberry bush," she would begin, hoping others would join in, "the monkey chased the weasel." She would sing and clap her hands. She had added a new ending.

"*POP-POP-POP-POP* goes the weasel."

We would arrive in time for Sunday school, and since Ed was teaching I kept Gram with me. We'd find a seat, and as Gram greeted all who passed by with a warm, hearty "Good morning," I would have the sinking feeling that I had been here before. We would sit together, and when Ed told us to turn to a particular passage, she would begin to do so.

Gram had read through the Bible more times in the previous fifteen years than anyone I knew. She and Flip would sit down in the morning and read from Proverbs or Ecclesiastes. But she was no longer able to find the passages.

She would interrupt the class, "What did Edward say, Mary? Was that Romans?"

By that time he had gone on to something else. In time, I had her look on with me, but I could not keep her from talking out loud in class. If she were a child, I could have escorted her to the nursery, but there was nowhere to go. I never knew what she was going to say next.

One morning a gentleman in class, sitting directly across from us, was speaking at length about something pertaining to the lesson. It appeared he didn't like to wear his dentures.

Gram reached over and turned my head towards hers, saying quite loudly, "My, Mary, he hasn't a tooth in his mouth—and look at the size of that belly!"

And this was only Sunday school class.

We'd head upstairs before church. Often someone would take me aside.

"Isn't it wonderful that your grandmother is so pleasant all the time?"

I would smile. Gram would spot Ed, grab his arm, and stay close beside him. She introduced him to anyone interested, although they were all well acquainted with him.

As they approached the pastor, she proudly introduced him, "This is Edward Walsh," she said.

The pastor smiled, and Ed smiled back.

"I know Edward, Mrs. Walsh—and how are you?"

"And I'm Laura; I'm his daughter!"

We entered the sanctuary, and Ed seated Gram at his side. He was usually able to keep her quiet unless she heard the word *introduce*. One morning, the pastor asked if there were any visitors to be introduced. She grabbed Ed's arm to raise it high in the air. He pulled it down.

"Don't you want me to introduce you, Edward?" she said out loud.

"Gram! Shhhhh."

✠   ✠   ✠

The thirty-minute ride home was a replay of the thirty-minute ride to church. Although it was extremely tense, I had no idea how much Ed's presence in the car meant until the day he stayed after church and I drove the family home without him.

It seemed that Gram realized the head of the house was not present, so she needed to take control. Every few seconds she would come up with an emphatic instruction for me or one of the children, and if she didn't get a response, she repeated it again and again. It became absolutely impossible for me to drive. I pulled off the highway onto the shoulder and told her she would have to be quiet or we would have an accident.

"I won't say another word!" she would insist.

If only that were possible, I thought to myself.

I made up my mind to never drive alone with her again.

We always ate together on Sundays, though I knew that we would face an uncomfortable situation following the meal. Gram would insist on washing the dishes, although she no longer believed it necessary to use soap. I would suggest that I wash and she dry—but she would become even more indignant.

I was so weary at times that I was simply too tired to argue. I would leave the kitchen, deciding I would just redo all the dishes later. There seemed to be no way to convince her without her becoming angry or insulted.

One Sunday afternoon, the house at last was quiet. Ed and I were in our bedroom talking. He was lying on the bed with his head on the pillow, and I was stretched out in reverse with my feet resting on my pillow. Looking back, I think I simply wanted to feel that I still had control of something in my life.

I heard Gram's footsteps on the stairs. She walked into our bedroom still fully dressed from church.

"Hi, Gram," Ed said.

She stood looking at me lying opposite Ed.

"Mary, turn around and put your head up on the pillow," she insisted.

"Oh, Gram, I'm just relaxing like this."

She planted her hands firmly on her hips.

"I said, put your head up on the pillow!"

"Gram," Ed said, "Don't talk to Mary like that."

She looked at us both with yet more resolve.

"That's my job!" she said emphatically as she clapped her hands together.

She turned, walked out the door, and headed back down the stairs.

✠   ✠   ✠

Sunday had become anything but a day of rest. It had become the most unrestful day of the week.

$\mathcal{B}$IRTHDAY $\mathcal{P}$ARTY—$\mathcal{A}$PRIL 1991   *10*

$\mathcal{A}$s the six little boys filed off the bus at noon, I savored the priceless moment. Still a bit awkward "on their own" in their big, new world—teeth missing in pairs, charming smiles—they were, no doubt, every bit as excited as David was. It was his birthday, and we had planned a special party for the occasion. Spring had finally arrived, and the sun, so long absent, warmed the little brood.

"Can we take our jackets off, Mom? It's really hot!"

"Sure, Dave. I may have to get the hose out if it gets much hotter!"

We pulled into the driveway, and almost before I could stop the car, they were gone, running toward the house to shed their school clothes. We began to play the games we had planned, but by the end of the party, the children had come up with one of their very own.

I had not mentioned the party to Gram but planned to invite her up with Flip when I served the cake. David was a little anxious about her coming upstairs because he was afraid she might do something unusual. Well, she did.

With everyone seated, I lit the candles on the cake and walked slowly toward David at the head of the table. I opened my mouth to begin singing "Happy Birthday," but before I could as much as get out the first syllable, Grandma began to sing, clapping her hands and dancing around the table.

"Happy birthday to you! Happy birthday to you!"

She marched round and round, smiling at David all the time. David rolled his eyes in embarrassment. I'm sure his little friends had never heard this rendition of "Happy Birthday" before. Their heads turned sharply each time she passed behind them.

"Gram! It's time for David to blow out his melting candles!" I yelled above her singing.

She stopped long enough for him to blow them out but started up again.

"Laura, let's go back downstairs!" Flip prodded.

The boys began eating their cake warily, but as Gram extended her hands to begin clapping and singing again, they pushed aside their cake and ran outside.

"Let's play 'Get away from Grandma!'" yelled little Travis as he bolted out the front door.

It was not cruel. It was simply their way of handling a very bizarre situation. Gram laughed and followed them outside. I trailed behind her, encouraging her to go back downstairs with Flip so the boys could finish their party, but she was having too much fun.

Later, when Ed arrived home, he asked David how his party went.

"We had fun, but Gramma—oh boy!" he said shaking his head.

I told Ed what had happened, and he motioned for David to come and sit beside him on the couch.

"I'm sorry that happened, Dave, but I want you to try to remember something for me."

"OK, Daddy."

"I know that it's hard, but try to remember," he continued, "that even though Gram does some silly things, some not so silly, she is still the same person she always was. She can't help it, David."

Ed often reminded us of our need to show compassion when we most wanted to throw up our hands in frustration. I knew he was feeling a sense of great personal loss as she gradually lost touch with reality. We were gradually losing her at the same time.

$\mathcal{N}$EGATIVE $\mathcal{E}$FFECTS   *11*

$\mathcal{A}$s Grandma's condition worsened, I became concerned for my children. How would her deterioration affect them, and how long would it go on? Yes, we had promised Gram we would not place her in a nursing home. As time went on, I would wrestle with our commitment. At what point did our children's needs take priority over this promise? One Scripture verse would often come to mind. It was from Psalm 15.

> WHO MAY WORSHIP IN YOUR SANCTUARY, LORD? WHO MAY ENTER YOUR PRESENCE ON YOUR HOLY HILL? THOSE WHO . . . KEEP THEIR PROMISES EVEN WHEN IT HURTS.   PSALM 15:1, 4, NLT

Wouldn't the Lord sustain us through this experience, wishing to honor our word and our grandmother? I found these answers were not coming easily.

There were some obvious negative effects on three-year-old David. Although he loved Gram living downstairs at first, as her behavior became gradually more bizarre, he began to get annoyed at her constant trips upstairs to "check on him." While she was still able to shop, she would bring home numerous bags of candy each week—small candy bars, chocolate-coated peanut butter cups, chewy candy, hard candy. I had always been careful not to give the children much candy.

David would come upstairs with pockets filled with candy.

"David, where did you get all that candy?" I would ask.

"Gramma gave it to me," he'd reply, spitting a mouthful of chewy caramel and chocolate into his hand so he could get the words out. I realized, of course, that giving candy to a grandchild is just part of being a grandparent. A treat is their privilege, but this had become excessive.

At first, I went down to speak with her.

"Gram, I know you want to be kind to David, but please do not give him candy without my permission."

"Oh, darling, I just gave him a few."

"Nevertheless, please ask me first."

The next time he came up with fists full of candy, I tried again.

"Gram, please, I asked you not to give David candy. It's not good for him!"

Sometimes she would get offended. "I'll never give him another piece!"

If I left the house for a few hours, I would come home only to find that she had given him candy. I would ask her not to buy it as she left for the store, but she would come home with the same incredible supply.

"I told her not to buy it, but she wouldn't listen," Flip would say, throwing her hands in the air.

"Ed, we have to do something. Gram will not stop giving David candy—lots of it!"

Ed attempted to reason with her, but it was futile.

One afternoon, upon discovering David's pockets bulging with candy, he resorted to flushing the entire basket of candy down the toilet. It took several flushes and a plunger as I recall.

"There, that solved the problem!"

Until the next shopping day.

And there is a price to pay for all things.

I was in tears, sitting in the waiting room of an oral surgeon's office a year later, as the doctor extracted two heavily decayed molars from my youngest son's mouth. I felt like a negligent mother, yet I did not even attempt to explain how this happened. How could I begin to explain what it was like to deal with someone I could no longer reason with?

I left the office feeling very frustrated at the lack of control I had in my own home.

The Coming Winter   12

As I struggled to take care of Gram—as our family struggled—something dark began to happen in our protected corner of the world. A darkness in thought—wrapped up in black and swastikas—began to manifest itself. It seemed as though we were facing a new threat.

I heard a recent statistic that in 1995, more than sixty-five neo-Nazi supremacist groups were active in Pennsylvania alone. In the fall of 1991, I must have assumed that groups such as these were most likely found in bigger cities—certainly not in a rural area like ours. I would soon learn how very, very wrong I was.

My first encounter with this disturbing element of our new hometown was at the local mall. As I walked through the entrance one September evening, I found myself in the very midst of a group of young men. I first noticed their black Doc Martin shoes. All of them were dressed in a similar manner—closely shaven heads, black flight jackets—not to mention various tattoos and piercings. As I was brushed aside by a younger member of the group, heading for the door, I caught a glimpse of a large black swastika displayed shamelessly across his chest. An older man followed closely at his heels, shaking his fists at them in rage. No doubt their Nazi symbols had set him off. I could scarcely recall my purpose for being there.

At the start of eleventh grade, Jamie began coming home with stories of racial tension at his high school. There had been an increasing influx of Black and Hispanic students from New York and New Jersey. Self-professed racists did not treat them—or any minority—with respect. Jamie was becoming increasingly upset—especially when a friend became the object of their taunts.

"Mom, they were making fun of Daniel today!" he told me. Daniel was born of an interracial marriage.

"Do you see that guy in there, Mom?" he asked me while at a nearby store. He was noticeably shaken.

"He's the one who threatened to kill me."

"What? Are you serious?" I asked. "Why?"

"Because I'm Daniel's friend," Jamie explained.

"Really, Jamie?"

"Really, Mom."

I was unable to take my eyes off that angry young man.

✠   ✠   ✠

Jamie had always been a reformer. If something was not right, he would do whatever he could to change it. One evening, he took matters into his own hands. The following day I received a call from the high school.

"Mrs. Walsh, I have your son Jamie in my office. He is being expelled from school. Would you come in, please?"

Lord, what now?

I entered the office and was shown posters Jamie had printed the night before, decrying racism, and posted on the halls of the school. One was similar to the no-smoking sign, a circle with a line through it over the word *racism,* meaning, No Racism. Another depicted the Ku Klux Klan, and it read, Ignorance is Contagious: End Racism. Others were less tasteful. Jamie told us later that a friend had done them. Jamie was responsible, nevertheless.

I was told that the posters were being misinterpreted, as if promoting racism. They had caused a disturbance. Jamie was expelled for the remainder of the school year.

I said little on the way home. I was angry. I could understand

Jamie's frustration, but expelled from school? I was sure Ed would have a lot to say on the matter, so I waited until we got home. Ed was angry.

"You're grounded! And don't ever use my printer again for something like that without consulting me."

Later that week, the family went to a nearby roller rink. It was a very nice family-oriented establishment, and we invited Jamie to come along with us. He skated over and pointed out a group of girls across the rink.

"Do you see those girls over there, Mom?"

I noticed several girls huddled together with the same short, straight, dyed black hair, wearing black flight jackets. They were staring back at us.

"They're part of the racist group in school."

"Well, just ignore them, Jamie."

Good advice—yet I soon found it to be difficult.

In their very center stood a woman in her late fifties. She began walking across the rink toward Jamie and Dawn, her arm extended stiffly in front of her, her hand raised. It was a familiar salute—a Nazi salute. It was evil.

"Seig Heil!" she shouted.

She stood staring at my children. Her eyes were cold and filled with hatred.

"Can you believe that, Mom? That's their grandmother!" Jamie said, shaking his head.

"This is America! Can anyone be so ignorant as to promote this again?"

All my reserve, my advice to ignore them, went out the window. As the group turned to leave the building, Jamie and I quickly untied our skates and left them with Dawn.

We ran through the parking lot toward their car. I tapped on the car window. The grandmother slowly rolled it down, a cigarette hanging loosely from her lips.

"How can you teach your children this hatred?" I demanded.

She laughed at me.

"You've raised a nigger lover!" she sneered.

"You are perpetuating this hatred in all these girls," Jamie said. "What's the matter with you?"

Not very long after this incident, the headline of the local paper showed further evidence that Jamie had not been exaggerating his concern. The headline read: "Skinhead Gets Life for Fatal Stabbing."

A twenty-year-old, self-described skinhead received a life prison sentence for fatally stabbing a man.

It was the same young man Jamie had pointed out to me—the one who had threatened his life. Although I prayed for them constantly, my children seemed at risk in many ways.

And Grandma's condition was worsening rapidly. Winter was at our door. That season would prove to be the roughest season of my life.

A Visit to the Dentist 13

$\mathcal{G}$ram lost a tooth—a front one. Although at a point where she was not really aware of it, we felt that if she were, she would want to have it taken care of.

When I called the dentist's office to make an appointment, I asked the receptionist to make a note regarding Gram's Alzheimer's. I wanted the dentist to be prepared for whatever might happen.

When Gram met the dentist, she greeted him with a smile so broad he didn't have to ask why we were there.

"I see you've lost a tooth, Mrs. Walsh!"

She continued to smile.

"My, but you're a handsome man! Don't you think so, darling?" she asked, looking over at me.

"Do you think you could sit in this chair, Mrs. Walsh, and we'll take a look to see what needs to be done?"

"My, what a lovely chair it is! Certainly!"

She positioned herself carefully in the chair, and as the dentist slowly lowered her head preparing to get to work, she looked intently up into his "handsome" face.

He took some impressions so he could have a partial plate made to replace her missing tooth. When he finished he raised the chair.

"We're all finished, Mrs. Walsh."

He instructed her to rinse her mouth thoroughly with water in the little paper cup by the side of the chair. She took a sip and turned to offer the cup to me.

"It's delicious, darling! Would you care for some?"

"No, thank you, Gram," I said. The assistant giggled. I'm sure this was a first.

"I'll call you as soon as your new partial plate comes in, and your smile will be good as new!"

"God bless you," she said as we left. "And you too, darling!" she said to the assistant.

By the time we received word from the dentist that the partial plate was ready, Gram's condition had deteriorated to a point where the plate was no longer necessary. She could not even brush her own teeth. "I'm so sorry to hear that," his receptionist said.

We paid for the plate but never even picked it up.

FRENZY **14**

$\mathcal{I}$ observed that prior to each major decline in Gram's condition, she would become extremely agitated and uncontrollable. I didn't know if this was common to all Alzheimer's victims or because of Gram's particularly strong will.

During the fall and winter months of 1991, her agitation reached a new high. She was not going to surrender willingly to this disease, but fight with every remaining ounce of mental and physical strength she possessed. At times we were caught in the crossfire of her desperate battle to ward off her enemy. Alzheimer's had met a formidable foe. But sadly, Alzheimer's always wins.

One chilly morning at dawn, I drew back the curtain, letting in a wintry sky—dark and pregnant with snow. School was canceled. There was a winter storm warning. The children rejoiced and returned to their beds, breathing sighs of relief. A sweet silence settled over the house as visions of drifting snow and a week of cancellations filled their heads.

The rustling of paper outside my bedroom door disturbed the stillness. I opened it a crack to discover several paper bags in a heap at the top of the stairs. Gram appeared moments later to deposit yet another one on the pile. She looked troubled.

"What are you doing, Gram?" I asked her.

"I'm going for the bus. I'm going home," she said with finality. Her words pulled my heart and stomach together, twisting
them into a tight knot. She turned to head back downstairs. She
had her heels on. She was dressed and ready to go.

"Gram, you are home. This is your home," I assured her. I
followed her. Once again, she was beyond the realm of words and
reasoning.

I walked over and peeked into one of the bags. They were
crammed with her clothes, not folded in any fashion but simply
stuffed into the bags, so uncharacteristic of the meticulous grandmother I knew.

I headed downstairs to her bedroom in time to see Flip frantically putting clothes back on hangers and into drawers.

"She empties them as quickly as I put them back!"

"Where is Margaretta? It's time to get the bus!" Gram
insisted.

"Gram, there is no bus; you are home," I reminded her.
"Let's bring your clothes back downstairs."

"I said, where is Margaretta?"

"I'm right here, Laura," Flip assured her.

"You are not Margaretta! She must be upstairs." Off she went.

Flip and I talked for a moment about this latest development.
I assured her I would help put all the clothes back, but we both
knew that would be the easy part. How we would convince Gram
that she was home and that there was no bus remained to be seen.

When we reached the top of the stairs, we were met with a draft
of cold air. The front door was wide open and Gram was nowhere
to be found. Running down the driveway we could see her through
the row of pine trees, walking swiftly down the middle of the road
carrying two of the shopping bags. A storm was imminent, but it
had become the lesser concern.

"You catch up with her, Flip, and I'll call Ed at the office." It
was yet another moment when I was thankful Ed's office was only a
few miles away.

"Ed! Gram is heading for Highway 209 to get the bus."

"What bus?"

"She thinks there is a bus to take her home. She's walking fast. You'd better head her off!"

"I'm going!" he assured me as he hung up.

I knew that if I went after her in my car there would be a scene, and I was not sure that I could get her into the car at all. If Ed showed up, she might calm down and listen to him. I waited anxiously at the end of the driveway and felt the first snowflakes on my bare arms—folded close to ward off the mounting wind.

Does she even have a sweater on? I thought to myself. *I don't think so.*

I watched Ed's car turn the corner—he had her. He pulled into the driveway and escorted Gram into the house. She was not happy.

"Gram, listen to me," Ed attempted to explain. "Remember, you live here. This is your home, and we love you. There isn't any bus!"

It was obvious Gram was not buying a word of it. She had determined—no matter what—that she would get to her bus and back home. Our home suddenly became a battleground; Flip and I were comrades in a mission to keep Gram from getting to the highway. The persistence she displayed over the following weeks was nothing short of incredible.

Gram interpreted my refusal to take her to the bus as unwillingness to help her. She was very insulted.

"Well, if you won't drive me to the bus, I'll just have to walk."

As I made an attempt to prepare dinner that evening, I glimpsed her scaling the hill outside the icy kitchen window. She was heading toward her car parked in the driveway.

By the time I ran outside and reached the car, she was inside frantically pulling switches, windshield wipers, and lights in an attempt to get it started. I pulled the door open.

"Jamie! Come and help me get Grandma!" I yelled through the stinging sleet.

He ran over, and we managed to get her out of the car and back into the house.

"You'd better hide the keys, Mom. If she ever gets it started, it will probably be her last ride!"

There were many doors in the house that lead outside, three of them on the downstairs floor. Gram tried them all. The following afternoon she slipped into her jacket, slung her pocketbook resolutely over her shoulder and, positioned for action, made her way to the side door. Flip caught her.

"Laura, stay inside!"

"I'm going for the bus. Leave me alone!"

I ran into the room in time to witness a fierce tug-of-war taking place with the pocketbook in front of the glass door. I had rarely heard Gram curse, but she had a few choice names that day for poor Flip, who appeared to have the edge. I squeezed behind Gram, forcing the door shut. Between the two of us we managed to walk her back into the living room.

She ran to the sliding glass doors and attempted to exit there, but Flip had placed a broken broom handle between the doors, which made it impossible to open. Flip came up with the most ingenious, makeshift locks that Gram could not figure out.

Gram ran over to the kitchen door and pulled it open with a vengeance. There was yet another unsuccessful attempt to reason with her, followed by some yanked hair—poor Flip. I marveled once again at the incredible physical strength Gram exerted. The two of us together could hardly budge her rigid body.

This chase between doors went on all afternoon—literally for hours. I cannot even recall how it stopped, but my guess is that Ed's arrival home somehow diverted her. She continued packing into the night, however, for her determined departure the following day.

Morning followed a restless night for all of us, but especially for Flip.

"Where is Margaretta? She must be at the house."

"I'm right here, Laura."

Flip stood somewhere between exasperation and exhaustion with a sign hanging from a string around her neck. On it she had printed in bold letters: I AM MARGARETTA.

☩   ☩   ☩

At times, in the midst of our mission, I forgot that my dear
comrade was eighty years old. Gram had ignored the reality of her
own age for a long time, along with concerns for her own aches
and pains.

"Take me to my house, Edward," she insisted. "My furniture
is there."

"Gram, your furniture is here." He walked her through the
rooms and pointed out all of her furniture.

"Who is in my house?" she demanded. "I must go and collect
the rent. Will you take me, Edward?"

Ed tried to explain again that we moved two years earlier and
sold her house—but she was not convinced.

"You stole my house!" she concluded, pacing the full length of
her living room.

I stood motionless in the midst of my home and family, now
turned upside down by the crisis. There was no end in sight. I
gazed out the window and watched the winter storm. Tree limbs
were laden with heavy snow, and it began to drift steadily deeper—
enclosing us in a world that had turned bizarre. Her words felt like
violent punches. I leaned on the couch, swallowing hard to hold
back tears.

Ed was speechless.

Had it really come to this?

What do we do now? Who do we call?

In desperation, I searched the phonebook for the Alzheimer's
Association. I was put in touch with a nurse who ran a home for
Alzheimer's patients. She had fifteen patients and special locks on
all outside doors to keep them from escaping. She could hear the
weariness in my voice—but I was beyond weariness. I was totally
astounded at the turn this disease had taken.

What were we going to do if this continued?

She explained the expense of keeping a patient with Alzheimer's—an amount we certainly could not afford. Medicare did not
provide funding for this type of facility. She kindly offered to take
Gram overnight, free of charge, to give us a rest.

Each day, Gram's agitation intensified. After several weeks, her determined effort to get to the bus shifted to a new and very desperate search—for her children. She began hearing her babies crying in the walls.

"They're back there—I have to get them!"

She determined that she could get into the wall through the electrical outlets and the best way to do that was with a very sharp knife. If she could just stick the blade into the outlet, she could get the babies out. I wrestled several knives from her hands. Flip hid them all, including butter knives. Ed called the doctor.

"Is there anything we can do to calm her down? She is totally out of control—her thoughts and actions are so bizarre. I'm afraid the next step will be a straitjacket."

"What do you mean by 'bizarre'?" the doctor asked. Ed told him of her most recent search for her children.

He prescribed a tranquilizer. Its result was that she climbed the stairs just as many times, but more slowly; her speech was slurred, yet she still asked the same strange questions. We were afraid she would fall down the stairs, so we discontinued the medication.

Gram would either end up on the highway or electrocuted if she succeeded in her "rescue missions." We needed to do something. We rigged up a belt through the back of the big lounge chair she always sat in, secured with a small lock. It was small, but it kept the belt secured. When we were not able to follow her around, we knew she was safe.

So now, Flip not only wore a sign around her neck, but a string with a key to the padlock. What a trooper!

At times I would pick up the phone to call a friend and try to explain what we were going through. I was hoping for relief to come from somewhere—but there were no words. I would hang up, realizing that the only one who could really understand was the Lord. I had the feeling that something was going to happen. The situation had reached such a peak of frenzy that something had to give way somewhere.

And it did.

MORE THAN HE BARGAINED FOR   15

*H*is little brown pickup pulling up the driveway was a welcome sight. Although he lived only twenty minutes away, I didn't see my brother Bruce often enough. When I did, it was nice to know that in this complex world, some people never change. He hopped out and began unloading his tools. He greeted me with his usual smile and a hug.

"Have some coffee before you get started?"

"That would be nice. Why don't you take me down first, and I'll take a look at the job?"

We called Bruce when we needed carpentry work done around the house. We had learned from experience that the price of hiring unknowns to do odd jobs could be expensive. Bruce was good, and I got to spend time with him. We were always close growing up, and it was nice to live in an area where we would occasionally run into each other. He was neat and worked fast, but no one could complete this job fast enough in my mind. It should have been done months earlier. We planned to enclose the stairs, installing a door with a lock at the bottom, believing it would deter Gram from climbing them all day long. We really had no choice.

He followed close behind as we walked down the stairway. Gram had met Bruce before, but I was quite sure she would not remember him.

"Gram, this is my brother Bruce. He's going to be working down here for a few days."

She smiled. "Hello! Aren't you a handsome man!"

"Why, thank you!" Bruce replied.

"Are you married?"

"Yes, my wife's name is Helen."

"Oh, that's lovely. Do you have any children?"

"Yes, I have two, Danny and Elizabeth."

"Oh, lovely! Where do you live?"

"I live in Tannersville, about twenty minutes from here."

"Gram, Bruce is the one who recorded those songs you like so much," I explained.

Bruce had recorded a number of original songs, and we often played his tape for Gram. She loved it. She would clap her hands and sing along.

"She's your biggest fan, Bruce!"

"My, but you are a handsome man."

"Why, thank you."

"Are you married?"

"Yes."

"Do you have any children?"

Bruce looked at me and grinned.

"Yes, their names are Danny and Elizabeth."

"Oh, lovely. Where do you live?"

"I live in Tannersville."

Bruce took his tape measure and began measuring for materials he would need. Gram continued the same round of questioning.

Bruce has a great sense of humor. He tried to have some fun with her and got pretty silly, but I secretly wondered how long he would be laughing. I knew he was in for an interesting few days.

"Let's go to Cramer's and pick up some materials," he said.

When we returned, Bruce went right to work.

Gram attempted her usual stair-climbing routine.

"Now, Grandma, you're going to have to stay off the stairs.

I've got wires and tools here you could trip over," Bruce patiently explained.

He was in for a surprise. If only it were that easy.

Up she came again.

And again.

"Laura, let's go into our room so Bruce can work," Flip finally suggested.

She and their sister Liz, who was up for a visit, walked Gram into the bedroom and shut the door.

Bruce went back to work. At least he thought he did.

"No, you can't go out there, Laura!"

"Oh, yes I can."

She began banging on the door.

Bruce looked at me, shaking his head in disbelief.

He continued working, but I knew it was not easy. Each morning over the next few days he was greeted by the same round of questioning, ascents up the stairs, and banging on the door. His jokes were fewer and farther in between.

The job took three days to complete. Well, almost. All that lacked was the lock, and that was out of stock. Bruce would install it as soon as it arrived.

✠   ✠   ✠

"Well, I've made my decision," Bruce announced as he packed up his tools.

"What's that, Bruce?"

"Helen and I are moving to Nashville."

"You're kidding!"

I knew that Bruce had been considering a move for several years, and Nashville would be the ideal place for his music to get exposure, but his announcement seemed so sudden.

"No, working here has made the decision for me. When I saw what has happened to Ed's grandmother, I realized I need to do this now. We just don't know what's ahead."

I tried to be excited. It was hard because I knew I would miss them, yet I realized all too well that there was truth in what he was saying. How often in God's Word we are reminded of the brevity of life.

> HOW DO YOU KNOW WHAT WILL HAPPEN TOMORROW? FOR YOUR LIFE IS LIKE THE MORNING FOG—IT'S HERE A LITTLE WHILE, THEN IT'S GONE.
>
> JAMES 4:14, NLT

He went home, put his house up for sale, and within a few months was gone. Although I miss Bruce and his family, it appears that the timing was perfect. They found a good church, and Bruce walked right into a job at Gibson Guitars as a luthier and designer. His talent is no longer a well-kept secret. His one-of-a-kind, hand-carved instruments have put smiles on the faces of some of Nashville's best musicians: Earl Scruggs, Kix Brooks, and Chet Atkins. Bruce will tell you to this day, "It is all because of Grandma."

His reaction was not unusual. Others shared that Gram's sudden and drastic decline made an impact on their lives. Our friend Nancy commented that Gram's striking, visible decline helped her come to terms with her own mortality.

✠   ✠   ✠

June 1993: The God Squad

I think back on those days—brand-new Christians so enamored by the hope set out in the gospel. We were on fire! All we wanted was to be used by God no matter what he might ask of us. We were so full of energy, and in our youthful, exuberant way we were shining for the Lord wherever and whenever we could.

What kind of examples were we now?

At times, while in the midst of various trials, I've often wondered if there is any light left there at all. And then two days ago, I had a wonderful thought. It came to me while in a most curious position. It was not a dream or a vision. I was in the bathroom. Actually, we were in the bathroom: Ed, Grandma, and me.

Picture this—we have it down quite well now. Ed holds Grandma up from behind, supporting her under the arms. I change the diaper, and Grandma fights us.

That's when it came to me. As I struggled to get those miserable tapes to stick while she struggled equally as hard to push my hands away, I thought, *They're here! The God Squad! They are right where God wants them to be at this moment in time.*

My World Upside Down   16

$\mathcal{E}$ven before opening my eyes, I sensed something unusual about the morning. A hollow, pleasant stillness enveloped the room. A small voice outside the door broke the stark silence.

"Mom, no school! We had lots of snow—it's a blizzard!"

As I reached over to shut off the alarm, I thought how nice it would be to sleep another hour. Before my hand left the clock, the entire room flipped upside down. I quickly shut my eyes and pulled the covers over my head.

"Oh no!"

"What's wrong, hon?" Ed asked.

"Something is very wrong," I said, holding my head between my hands. "Everything is spinning!"

I lay there trying not to move a muscle, my eyes closed. The spinning calmed down. But the moment I opened them, my world spun out of control again. The spinning caused immediate nausea and vomiting; the cycle continued for several hours.

The morning marked the beginning of the "Blizzard of '92." The turmoil that ensued within our four walls far surpassed any of the hardships we experienced.

The stairs were enclosed, and there was a door now—but the lock had not yet been installed.

Ed stayed home until the plows had cleared the road between

home and his office. The business was going well, and he was working long, hard hours. I worked with him, doing accounting and secretarial work. That was now impossible.

"Call me if you need me," he said as he left.

The dizziness had settled down, but I noticed if I moved my eyes to the left even slightly it immediately came on again. I was afraid to move.

"Mommy, can I get you anything?" Dawn asked.

"No, thank you, hon. Hopefully I'll be up soon."

She pulled the door shut behind her. Within seconds it opened again.

"Where's Mary?" Gram asked, walking into the room.

"I'm here, Gram," I said, cautiously trying not to move.

"I'm going to look for Margaretta. Maybe she's out here."

She headed for the sliding glass door that led to the snow-covered deck.

I raised my head in time to see her walk outside.

"Gram, she's not there. Please come inside."

The sudden movement triggered a new cycle of dizziness, nausea, and vomiting. I managed to call Chris. He retrieved Grandma and escorted her downstairs.

Moments later she was on the stairs again, this time with Flip trailing behind her.

"Laura, stay down here! Mary's sick; she needs to rest."

"Oh, leave me alone."

I could sense a struggle between them on the stairs. I pictured one or both of them falling down.

The trips up and down into my room continued. If my door was locked, she would pound on it.

"Mary, let me in!"

"Gram, please go downstairs. I'm so sick. Please!"

I managed to reach the phone and call the office.

"We have to do something. Call Bruce. Is that lock in?"

I knew he would not be able to get to our house because of the snow. Ed called him anyway.

"The lock won't be in until Monday. I'll get there as soon as I can."

I have no idea how many trips she made during those hours.

I heard her on the stairs again, assuring Flip she would be right back. I'm not sure what the purpose of the trip was this time, but as she headed back down, I heard her trip and fall with several loud thumps before landing flat on her back on the bottom step.

"Oh, my back! Oh!" she cried.

I forced myself to my feet. Staggering and reeling with dizziness, I headed toward the stairs. Leaning heavily on the banister, I made my way to the bottom.

Somehow we got her to the couch.

"Look, you made Mary come down," Flip scolded. "Now will you stay down here?"

"Grandma," I said firmly. "Stay down here!"

Maybe if I could say something with finality—maybe if she knew I was angry—she would listen.

Looking back, I see this moment as the turning point. My reserve strength was gone. Physically, I was giving way. I spent the next three days in bed.

When I was finally able to get up, my equilibrium was not right. Fluorescent lighting, crowded food stores, driving in traffic—all threatened to trigger another attack. I felt extremely anxious.

The doctor provided a name for my ailment: vertigo. The only treatment available was the medication used for treating carsickness. It was not very effective for me. A possible cause was a minute particle of something in my inner ear canal. The doctor suggested that I make myself dizzy, moving my head back and forth to bring on an attack which might force the particle out. That was a tall order.

I asked how long it might last.

"Weeks, months—possibly years."

My condition returned every few months: three days in bed followed by weeks of recovering—all the while feeling the effects. I was to suffer from this for over two years.

Gram's trips up the stairs had ended. She lay on the couch holding her back, wondering why it hurt so much.

The lock was installed on the door, but it was like closing the barn door after the horse has escaped. We knew it would be necessary when she felt ready to start climbing again.

AFTER THE LOCK   17

The lock was definitely a good idea. It had a push-button combination. When anyone went downstairs, he or she would quickly shut the door and set the lock. Often Gram would be waiting to get upstairs, so quick action was essential. She had no idea there was a combination; she just knew she was not able to open the door.

There was, however, a small problem we had not anticipated. It often happened very early in the morning.

Bang! Bang! Bang! Bang! Bang! Bang!

"Laura, Stop that!"

Bang! Bang! Bang! Bang! Bang! Bang!

Ed would go down and try to calm her or bring her upstairs for a while.

✠   ✠   ✠

Suddenly, there came a big change in Gram. One morning, she had no desire to get up. She had always been an early riser, but on this day she wanted to stay in bed. She lay trembling in her bed, her speech noticeably affected. We thought she might be dying. She finally did get out of bed, but there was a definite decline and change in her condition.

She was now content to sit in her chair and was less agitated. She was gone. She would still smile, but she no longer sang. At this point, she began her counting. She would count on her fingers to one hundred, day in and day out. Even during the night she could be heard searching for the next number, "ninety-six, ninety-seven, ninety-eight . . ." pausing only to search her memory for the numbers she could not remember.

The frenzy had passed, and the tremendous change in her condition brought with it the realization that she was nearing the end. It seemed that there might be peace at long last, however bittersweet, in the Walsh home.

$\mathcal{B}$ROKEN $\mathcal{D}$REAMS

"$\mathcal{M}$rs. Walsh, this is Miss Jacobs. I'm a guidance counselor at the high school. I have your son Chris sitting across from me. We've been talking, and I'm recommending the possibility of foster care for him."

My heart pounding wildly within my chest, I tried my best to restrain my immediate response. I felt almost overcome with the sentiment often alluded to in Scripture, that of a bear robbed of her cubs.

> LIKE A BEAR ROBBED OF HER CUBS, I WILL ATTACK THEM AND RIP
> THEM OPEN.   HOSEA 13:8, NIV

"You what?" Surely I had misunderstood.

"What do you mean? He's our son! You have no right to make such a recommendation, not knowing anything about the situation."

"Well, Mrs. Walsh, you know at age fifteen it is a toss-up as to whom Christopher belongs, you or the state."

This was only the first of the jolts that were ahead for us.

There had been many indications that our son was troubled. His behavior had radically changed over the past several months. He involved himself with friends who appeared equally troubled and grew alienated from our family. One month earlier, we had taken him out of his private school because he was depressed and unhappy. With great reservation, we placed him in the local high school.

That morning I asked him to stay home so we could discuss several issues left unresolved the night before. I feared if he left without a resolution, he would not come home afterward.

When I checked his bedroom, he was gone and had taken some clothing and his toothbrush. A sick chill rushed through me. A moment of anger gave way to anxiety and a feeling of great loss. I was sure he had run away.

I immediately called the police.

"I'm afraid my son has run away from home," I blurted out, not wishing to believe my own words.

"Can you give us a description: height, weight, what he is wearing?"

I described his height and weight, his clothing and backpack. They could have picked up any one of a thousand kids using my description.

"Does he have any distinguishing features—scars?"

"Yes, he has red hair," I added. *Beautiful red hair*, I thought to myself.

When I received the call from the guidance office, I was at first relieved that he was not headed across the country. Yet I realized we, as parents, had become the bad guys. We felt we needed to defend ourselves.

He did not return home after school, and we began a futile search to find him. I called all his friends.

"Mrs. Johnson, this is Mrs. Walsh, Christopher's mother. I wonder if you or your son have seen Chris today?"

"No, I haven't seen him. My son hasn't seen him either."

"Please, if you hear from him or hear where he is, please call me!"

"Yes, I will."

I spent nights waiting to hear from him.

"I cannot imagine a child loved and raised in a Christian home becoming a teenager and rebelling against his parents—how could that be?" It was a question that we had often posed as young parents—long before Christopher left.

My journal entries recorded this story for three years—as we painfully learned firsthand that it was indeed possible. He was a runaway for over three months during that time. When he was apprehended and brought home by the police, he was unrepentant. The tension and disruption that he brought home with him was almost unbearable.

He went so deep into his rebellion that he became hardened and unreachable. I lost hope that he would ever really return.

Throughout this heartrending, emotionally draining time, Grandma's disease continued its rapid and cruel ravage of her mind. I could not say, "Hold it! My heart is breaking, my son is missing."

She could not understand. She had her own torments to contend with, and there were few answers anywhere to be found.

✠   ✠   ✠

I sought the help of a Christian counselor. He recommended the book *Parents in Pain* by John White.

I also picked up a book called *Tough Love.* The author describes a scene of weary, heartbroken parents sitting across from a counselor. The parents, who have endured many sleepless nights and confrontations, now appear as a frazzled, borderline neurotic couple. As the meeting progresses and emotions mount, the counselor concludes, "No wonder this child has problems."

This was almost an exact description of our first meeting with a counselor.

In the first session—which did not go well—we told Chris that we loved him and wanted him to come home. The counselor mediated. Chris would have to abide by the rules of our home. This was the stumbling block. We made it clear to him that if he chose not to come home, the police would be called, and he would be picked up. At fifteen, a minor, it is against the law for him to be on his own.

My heart sank once again as he turned from us as if a stranger, walking off down the road into the wintry night. His black leather jacket swallowed up by the darkness, he quickly disappeared from our sight.

So defiant, so young, and so unaware.

It hurt so much to watch him walk away.

CHRISTOPHER: "CHRIST BEARER"   *19*

> BUT OH, MY DEAR CHILDREN! I FEEL AS IF I AM GOING THROUGH
> LABOR PAINS FOR YOU AGAIN, AND THEY WILL CONTINUE UNTIL
> CHRIST IS FULLY DEVELOPED IN YOUR LIVES.   GALATIANS 4:19, NLT

I thought back sixteen years to a drizzly summer morning. A silhouette of light surrounding the overcast sun peered through the bedroom curtain.

"I'm only a phone call away," Ed reminded me, resting his hand gently on my very large tummy as he leaned over to kiss me good-bye.

"Maybe today is the day!" The thought of our second child being born was all the sunshine he needed. I knew that my labor was imminent.

Jamie bounced around the room anxiously, aware that the morning had not begun according to our usual routine. Yet he was not sure of the big event ahead.

"Mommy, get up! It's time to get up!"

My mother appeared at the door to escort Jamie out for breakfast. Dozing off for a short time, I was awakened by intense contractions in quick succession. I was convinced that this would in fact be the day.

The hospital was close to fifty minutes away. Ed would need at least thirty minutes to get home. I reached for the phone.

"Please tell Ed Walsh that he should leave for home—now."

What seemed to be only minutes later, his truck pulled up the driveway, and he appeared at my side.

"Did you fly?" I asked.

"You bet. Let's go!"

We said our good-byes and I grabbed some necessary belongings. Nervously scattering instructions here and there as Ed hustled me out the door, my mom followed close behind snatching each one up.

"Jamie will be fine! Don't worry about a thing."

I had never been away from him for more than several hours at a time. Would he really survive without me?

The rain beat heavily on our little Volkswagen. It had certainly seen better days, but I felt confident it would get us to the hospital. We'd need a replacement in the near future for sure. We would now be a family of four. I felt more confident this time, having attended Lamaze classes with Ed. We were convinced by our first encounter in the labor and delivery room that we could use all the help we could get.

✟   ✟   ✟

"How about Matthew Edward?" I suggested in between contractions. We had not quite decided on a name.

"Don't you think there have been enough Edwards in the family?" asked Edward III.

"But it would be his middle name; I would hate to break a tradition."

Very few girls' names came to mind. I felt sure we would have another son. When we arrived at the hospital the rain was still falling heavily.

"I'll let you out here and park the car," Ed said as he pulled up to the emergency entrance. That was a big mistake. The next contraction was so hard I could not hide the pain. A nurse ran out behind a wheelchair and escorted me to the elevator and up to the labor room. Ed followed soon after.

My doctor appeared. Upon examination he gave me a bit of advice.

"Go home and read a good book, like *Gone with the Wind.*"

I assured him that I was in labor and I could not go home. He assured me that he was the doctor, and *Gone With the Wind* was an excellent book.

With that he left the room.

"I know my wife, and she's no sissy. If she says she is in labor, I have to believe her."

The nurse gave us a sympathetic look, shrugging her shoulders in resignation.

"We'll be back!" Ed assured her.

We made our way back to the elevator, down to the entrance, stopping every five minutes or so for a contraction. I sat while Ed disappeared into the heavy rain to get the car. I'm sure those who saw us wondered what was wrong with this picture.

I slid into the backseat of the cramped little car and lay on my side, panting and breathing to relieve the pain. We had agreed there was no way we could go all the way home, so we drove until Ed stopped the car in the midst of an old car graveyard. Surrounded by rusting metal shells of one-time fancy dreams, seats of tattered upholstery, and balding tires, our little car fit in beautifully. It would go unnoticed.

Within the hour it became obvious that this baby was about to make his appearance. Then a police car pulled up. The officer approached us, pulling down his visor to shield his face from the downpour. He tapped on the window with his flashlight. "What is going on here?"

I think he suspected we were parking. A quick glance behind the seat to see me, great with child, panting during an especially hard contraction, relieved any such suspicions.

Ed explained our plight.

"I'll wait over at the entrance and when you're ready, I'll escort you. Don't wait too long!"

Within a few minutes we were on our way. The officer motioned for us to follow. Actually, I think he was much more excited than our doctor was. At least he believed me.

I don't really remember much about the ride back to the hospital. But I do recall the doctor's face when he saw me rushed to the delivery room. He must have thought I was a speed-reader.

Within a very short time our son was born—a tough, feisty little redhead.

Redhead?

Our joy was heightened by surprise. We never expected a redhead to be born to a brown-eyed, dark-haired couple. As the days passed he became even more beautiful. One of the nurses named him "Rosebud" and asked if she could take him home.

We named him "Christopher," meaning "Christ bearer."

✠   ✠   ✠

From the journal of Mary Walsh
November 1994

I spent the night in the most intense travail for my son. He has been gone for over two weeks. I've been pleading with the Lord to do a work in his heart. It is as if I have been in travail again until Christ is formed in him. Of course it is only the work of the Holy Spirit that can humble his stubborn heart; until then, I feel the same longing for that moment. The pain of watching my child rebel, the hurt as he runs away from our home and protection, is far deeper and more intense than any of the pains of childbirth.

$\mathscr{J}$ust $\mathscr{S}$nap $\mathscr{O}$ut of $\mathscr{I}$t  20

For weeks before his admission to the hospital, my father experienced an extended period of depression.

"How can he be depressed?" a well-meaning, but misguided friend asked my mother. "He's a Christian!"

Not long after my father entered the hospital, it was discovered that his kidneys had failed, filling his blood with poisons and impurities. He was a very sick man; dialysis treatment was ordered immediately. The doctor assured my mother that his depression was most likely caused by the kidney failure.

We often seem to disregard the fact that our emotional well-being is closely related to the condition of our physical bodies.

Snap out of it. That is often the advice for those suffering from depression, as if by their will they actually could. Having enjoyed excellent physical health all of my life, I was among those who never made the connection.

Another erroneous preconceived notion was about to take a nosedive.

✠   ✠   ✠

SAVE ME, O GOD, FOR THE WATERS HAVE COME UP TO MY NECK. I
SINK IN THE MIRY DEPTHS, WHERE THERE IS NO FOOTHOLD. I HAVE
COME INTO THE DEEP WATERS; THE FLOODS ENGULF ME. I AM WORN

OUT CALLING FOR HELP; MY THROAT IS PARCHED. MY EYES FAIL,
LOOKING FOR MY GOD.   PSALM 69:1-3, NIV

My body was as heavy as lead. I felt as if I would melt through the floor, and that the earth would open up and swallow me. Strangely enough, I almost welcomed my disappearance. My limbs were so heavy and felt so detached from my body that I could not move them. Every beat of my heart reverberated throughout my body.

Where did the time go? There was no time.

I was sinking deeper and deeper into trouble. I wanted to cry for help, but I couldn't. Was I dreaming?

Did I need an ambulance—or perhaps an undertaker?

If I moved to turn to my left, vertigo would strike.

As I think back, a time frame escapes me. I'm not sure if I was in bed for days or weeks—it seemed like months.

I went to my doctor the day I began experiencing symptoms of a heart attack. I ended up at a neurologist who scheduled an MRI.

Ed and I sat across from him explaining my symptoms. After extensive questioning, he performed some simple tests in the office, checking my balance as I walked, my vision, my physical strength.

"I want to do a brain scan. Your symptoms could indicate multiple sclerosis or a brain tumor."

He could not find any other cause for the reoccurring vertigo, depression, and physical weakness I was experiencing.

The following week was spent in and out of bed. While up, I forced myself to go through the motions of living. I'm sure I must have cooked and cleaned and taken care of Gram, but all is vague.

I was so convinced I was dying—so profoundly depressed—that I wrote notes to my daughter and mother, "In the event that I die." (I never actually gave them to them.)

✠   ✠   ✠

FROM THE JOURNAL OF MARY WALSH
December 1993
Around September I experienced a complete physical and

emotional collapse. I became totally depressed to the point of taking medication. I also began to experience episodes of vertigo again, so I've gone through a series of tests and should have the results Thursday. The tests are to rule out MS and a brain tumor.

It is very strange to be awaiting the results. At times I'm strong, at times I'm afraid. I really pray the results would rule out both. I would love to be healthy again and see my children grow— David is so young. Yet I realize, all is in the Lord's hands.

The scan did not indicate MS or a brain tumor, for which I was very thankful.

I now believe that my body had simply broken down, physically and emotionally, as a result of the extended periods of stress and the jolts I had experienced over the recent years. It took me a full six months to recover.

Ed would take me for walks in the woods on weekends, and I remember the effort of each step as if a severe flu had weakened me. It was painful to talk about anything serious, so I did not talk much at all. I cried very easily.

Very gradually I regained my physical and emotional stability. I found, however, that it had left me with a weak point, and just as a sprained ankle must be favored after a sprain, I had to be on my guard and really pray and fight the downward pull of depression. Its threat hovered over me at all times.

FROM THE JOURNAL OF MARY WALSH
July 1994

We took Gram to see her doctor. It was an emergency visit. We are sinking, and help seems so far off. I told him of my desire to place her in a home. He nodded in agreement.

"She needs three nurses around the clock," he said, shocked

at her decline this time. "However the wait may be three to six months."

I am only one person.

I had renewed strength because I could see this hope even afar off. I'm praying as I have asked others to pray that the Lord would intervene and have mercy.

As we sat in the waiting room, a gray haired woman read a magazine beside me.

"What are you reading, Margaretta?" Gram asked her.

The woman didn't look up.

"I said, 'What are you reading, Margaretta?'"

She continued turning pages.

"I'm appalled at her," Gram said quietly with disgust.

✠   ✠   ✠

I walked her outside in a wheelchair to avoid any further disturbances. A heavyset woman walked by. I couldn't turn her chair away fast enough.

"She should have stayed home today; she's a mess!"

✠   ✠   ✠

We didn't skip through the parking lot this time.

"Pop Goes the Weasel" is now a forgotten tune.

It took both Ed and me to get her to the car.

FROM THE JOURNAL OF MARY WALSH
August 1994

This has been the start of a new era. Hip is no longer able to help in the care of Grandma. I am now the primary caregiver. There is little help anywhere. I contacted the Aging Office. I'm waiting for a program provided by the state instead of resorting to a nursing home. I found one that offers an hour each morning, five days a week, plus several hours on one day. For the remaining twenty-three hours each day they have Mary Walsh written down. The hardest part is realizing I cannot leave.

The help they sent yesterday was unable to handle Gram.

"This is not a one-person job," she told me. So I assisted her.

Ed was gone all day at the hospital with Flip. She is to undergo surgery.

Gram was uncooperative, and I struggled with her. Bitter, angry—I fell into a deep depression. I really discouraged Ed when he came home. As a team we can get through, but I certainly abandoned him yesterday.

I woke up this morning—vertigo, weak—realizing if I continue in this downward cycle, I'll be back where I was six months ago.

I was helped greatly by some words written by Amy Carmichael in the midst of her trials:

In acceptance there lies peace.

All the paths of the Lord are loving and faithful.

All does not mean all except the path I am walking on now, or nearly all except this especially painful path.

All must mean all.

I am resting my heart on the word.

It bears me up on eagle's wings.

It gives courage and song and sweetness too.

That sweetness of spirit which is death to lose even for a half hour.

The evil whisperer never forgets to come, whispering his appeal to that persistent "I." How good it would be to be free of these circumstances. When will that day come? How long it is in coming. . . . No, he never forgets to torment.

But I have found a definite and swift deliverance, in turning to Him who is nearer than any whisper. I say instantly, "Make peace the inmost desire of my heart."

Then there flows into me peace, and with it the assurance of the beloved. However things may appear to be, of all possible circumstances in whose midst I am set, these are the best that He could choose for me. We do not know how this is true, where would faith be if we did? But we do know that all things that happen are full of shining seed.

Light is sown for us, not darkness.

(Amy Carmichael, Rose from Briar)

The Lord Sent Laura ## 21

$\mathscr{I}$ was informed by the Office of Aging that a new program was about to begin for Gram. She would be cared for one hour each morning, five mornings a week, by a hospice organization. Just hearing the word *hospice* brought home the fact that Gram was possibly nearing the end of her struggle.

The Lord knew that we needed some encouragement. Although all the nurses were pleasant and helpful, the Lord sent Laura to encourage us in a very special way.

She was bubbly, obviously in love with her work and her patients. She loved Grandma instantly. They even shared the same name. Flip and I looked forward to her visits. She would spend time with Gram, helping her to write her name, fixing her hair, talking to her. Gram would smile and tell her she was lovely. She would often tell me about her other patients.

"I have a patient, Mrs. Cohen, she's 104 years old. Every day she wakes up, looks around, and says, 'I'm still here?!'"

We would laugh together. I soon found that she was a Christian, and we could share some not-so-pleasant stories. I opened up and told her about the heartache we were going through with our son Christopher. She shared some of her struggles as a divorced mother of three children.

She loved working with the terminally ill, as difficult as that was. She would update me each day with tears in her eyes. Often she would point them to Christ during their final days.

One day she came with a heavy burden of her own. Her checkup at the doctor had revealed a diagnosis of breast cancer, and she would need immediate treatment and surgery. She was only thirty-seven. Over the next months she went through some very difficult times. She shared how painful it was to stand in front of a mirror and brush clumps of her long, thick black hair from her head. She was forced to wear a wig. She still smiled and made Grandma laugh. Very little time was lost, although one week she was so terribly sick after a treatment that she could not make it.

One day she came and told me that someone in her office had found fault with her revealing to her patients the fact that she had cancer. I had a hard time understanding this. She had been such an example to me throughout her very difficult time. I would have missed out on her encouragement had she hidden it from me. Often, seeing someone living genuinely through suffering and weakness can make the most profound impression; witnessing firsthand "Christ's strength made perfect in weakness."

While waiting in the doctor's office one day with Gram, I picked up a pamphlet entitled "Understanding and Living with Alzheimer's Disease." As I read portions of it aloud to Ed, in between attempting to restrain Gram's comments, we snickered, filling in the between-the-lines information that the pamphlet did not cover. The pamphlet was very informative, but it is impossible to convey what it is like to live with this disease in only fourteen pages. I took it home and added some bits of information from our experience that might paint a clearer picture.

> To alleviate the stress that accompanies caregiving, families should explore hobbies, interests, and other forms of diversion.

I suppose it was due to the extreme nature of the stress we were under that our diversion was of such an extreme nature.

Our first hike to the top of the Delaware Water Gap began as a family venture with the children on a Saturday not long after we moved to Pennsylvania. We drove to the visitor's center at the bottom of the gap, parked the car, and decided to hike the white trail, which would take us to a lookout near the top. The ascent, a distance of about two-and-a-half miles climbing to an eight hundred-foot elevation was rugged; lots of rocks to climb and streams to cross, but it was pleasant. Jamie, then thirteen, took every opportunity to climb as high as we thought safe, or just a little higher. Chris followed close behind; Dawn stayed with me. The view at the top from the New Jersey side of the gap—the highway and Delaware River cutting through down below, hawks soaring at eye level—was breathtaking. We sat on the massive boulders and rested for a while—some of us did, anyway.

Our first descent was memorable.

"I think we'll take a shortcut down," Ed said as we followed close behind. All three children turned to look at me with the same look of horror.

"Shortcut?"

Shortcut had become an ominous word in our home over the years. This shortcut showed again that our fears were justified. We ended up on our behinds, sliding down a rockslide. The stains never did come out.

"Keep pumping, David. Cody would like some water, too," Ed prodded. David primed the pump at the water fountain at the base of the mountain.

Cody, our beautiful, cream-colored shepherd-lab mix dog, looked forward to our trips to the gap as much as we did. Just the sound of his chain leash being removed from the closet got his adrenaline pumping. He'd prance from one end of the house to the other like a young pup. He couldn't wait.

David leaned down on the pump handle with the weight of his entire body and then pulled up again with all his might. Cody stood waiting expectantly, his eyes fixed on the faucet.

"Uh . . . uh, David!" Ed finally blurted out. He was so shocked that he momentarily forgot his son's name. He yanked him out of the way of a large, coiled rattlesnake in striking position only inches from David's foot.

I had watched our dog, Cody, on a number of occasions grab a garter snake between his jaws and proceed to shake it until it was limp and lifeless. Anticipating his next move, I yanked his leash and ran across the gravel parking lot away from the rattlesnake.

Once Ed was satisfied that David was at a safe distance, he

stood aside and began to admire the sheer beauty of the creature—
a sentiment I had difficulty sharing.

"Mary, go tell some people to come if they want to see a rattlesnake," Ed yelled.

It was especially crowded that day, and Cody and I, intent on
sharing our discovery with some of the tourists, quickly realized
that none spoke English.

"Eddie, how do you say 'snake' in Spanish?" I called to him.

They came running as if they needed no interpreter. "Snake"
is the same in any language—sinister, sly, yet so intriguing.

A park ranger passing through stopped to take a look at the
snake that had become the focus of dozens of chattering visitors.

"You should feel very special," she said. "This is a black-faced
timber rattlesnake. You rarely see them here."

That was indeed good news. For Ed, that he got to see such a
rare beauty, and for me, that it was not likely we would be running
into another one.

Ed and I found that we could drive to the gap when he got
home from work, hike the five miles, and be back in time to help
Flip get Gram ready for bed.

As the trail became more familiar to us, we discovered
running up the trail was really fun. That was an element that had
been missing from my life for some time, though I was almost
afraid to admit it at first. It was a challenge because of the wild
nature of the trail—rocks, tree roots, and the fact that it was all
uphill.

At first we would run a short distance and then walk. As the
weeks passed we would run greater distances and walk in between.
By September we were running most of the way up and all the way
down. But this trail became more than an outlet for relieving the
stress in our lives; it became a very extraordinary place to both of
us.

From the time we first met, Ed had shared his almost romantic
attachment to the woods with me.

"Smell the moss, Mary. Isn't it wonderful?" The sight of wild
mushrooms would thrill him. He would get down on his knees to

take a closer look. I got more of a kick out of observing him than the mushroom.

"I love it here," he'd tell me, "because when we're here we can't be reached. There's no telephone. We're alone." His love for it all was highly contagious, and I learned to take great delight in the woods as well.

The gap became a haven where we would share our deepest thoughts—laugh and cry and pray. In time we came to see the trail much as we saw our lives; filled with obstacles to be overcome, with only a very occasional smooth spot.

At times I came away with some meaningful lessons, like the day I felt so good running down the trail, that I got ahead of Ed—way ahead. I began to feel a bit smug. I knew I'd reach the bottom long before him and be waiting at the waterfall. I could just picture his face! I kept running, until to my delight a little roly-poly black bear cub lumbered across the path in front of me. I stopped short.

I just have to wait for Ed, he's got to see this! I thought to myself. I called his name but realized he might not hear me until he got closer—after all, I had gotten way ahead of him. I suddenly realized as I stood looking around me that the trail looked unfamiliar—it was wide and unusually smooth. The woods were different—very dense—and the sky was beginning to turn dark. Was it a storm overhead, or was it later than I thought?

It finally occurred to me that Ed would not be coming. I was lost.

I remembered having once asked a ranger if black bears were dangerous. He assured me that "the only time you have to be concerned about running into a black bear is if you have food, or if you get between a mother bear and her cub."

It wasn't much comfort now, alone in the dark and unfamiliar woods—and having just seen the cub.

I walked quickly, hesitant to run, praying that I would meet Ed and not Mother Bear. I walked about half a mile before I ran into some hikers. I explained my plight, my smugness left far behind.

They directed me to a path that would eventually lead to the waterfall where I had hoped to be waiting for Ed.

I hoped he and Cody would be waiting there and had not decided to send a party out to search for me.

What a relief it was to see Cody basking in the waterfall, as was his custom after each run, and Ed waiting eagerly for me to make my appearance.

"What happened?" he asked as he hugged me. "Where have you been?"

"I guess I missed the turn," I cried. "We really need to stick together on this trail," I concluded. It was true here as well as in all we were going through.

> TWO ARE BETTER THAN ONE, BECAUSE THEY HAVE A GOOD RETURN FOR THEIR WORK: IF ONE FALLS DOWN, HIS FRIEND CAN HELP HIM UP. BUT PITY THE MAN WHO FALLS AND HAS NO ONE TO HELP HIM UP!
> ECCLESIASTES 4:9-10, NIV

☩ ☩ ☩

FROM THE JOURNAL OF MARY WALSH
July 1994

Wednesday evening we headed up the trail. I felt especially good. Walking felt great and running was OK too. The downhill trip is really challenging because of all the rocks and tree roots, but it's really fun because it is all downhill.

I was trying not to become careless but hit a small tree root, twisted my ankle, and fell. The next mile-and-a-half was unbelievable. There was no way I could walk, and it would soon be dark, so Ed carried me on his back the entire way down. It was steep and rocky. I called him my "hero."

I hope the sprain heals quickly and it's not the end of an era that has simply been fun and a break from the difficulties of life in the Poconos.

FROM THE JOURNAL OF MARY WALSH
July 1994

Flip may have had a stroke. She can't use her left hand. We feel at a loss. What next? We prayed together. Grandma has become difficult to manage again, and Flip is so worn out.

I had a moment of enjoying some special treatment "off my feet." "Mom, I'm your slave. I'll do whatever you want!" was David's reaction to my injury. Is this too good to be true, or what? But it was short lived! I have one good foot, and Flip, one good hand. We're still a team!

FROM THE JOURNAL OF MARY WALSH
July 1994

This evening I hobbled into the hospital with Flip. I returned home without her. She did have a stroke.

FROM THE JOURNAL OF MARY WALSH
July 1994

Ed had to sleep in with Gram for a number of nights, because of my ankle and inability to walk if she got up during the night. (She was delighted!) When Flip returned home from the hospital she would call us on an intercom between four and five in the morning. Ed and I would go down and take Gram to the bathroom, change her diaper, and put her back to bed.

"Did you ever dream it would come to this?" Flip cried one night.

I've tried to get help but it's difficult.

FROM THE JOURNAL OF MARY WALSH
September 1996

One day while sitting at the top of the gap, the pleasant and necessary refuge it had become really struck us.

"*Do you realize how many times we have come up here and poured out our hearts to the Lord? When Chris was gone, so many times for Gram, for my dad, not knowing if he'd live another day.*"

Yet every time we reached the top and sat above it all, the surrounding beauty overwhelmed us. There we could meet with the Lord and unload our overwhelming cares and concerns. Our closest times, no doubt, have been those moments when we realized once again that "*only the Lord is sufficient for these things.*"

The downhill stretch—with the renewed strength promised in Isaiah to "*those who wait on the Lord*"—became a piece of cake.

CHANGING ROLES $\quad$ 23

$\mathcal{I}$ sat and stared at the article on Alzheimer's. I read that sentence again.

> Caring for an Alzheimer's disease patient may require sacrifice, changes in priorities, and perhaps changes in roles for other family members.

Oh, boy, this is a good one, I thought to myself.

I think the word *perhaps* is a bit weak. The changes come gradually as the disease progresses, but they are very noticeable and can be quite unusual.

To sum up the changes of the roles in our household to date: Grandma has become the child requiring constant care, watching, dressing, and changing. Our children have become the "grown-ups" and Grandma-sitters. They try so hard to help ease her confusion, often to no avail. They have grown in their understanding of putting the needs of a helpless human being first. This did not come easily, but the fruit has now become evident in each of them.

Edward has become Grandma's husband. Grandma will grab Ed and hug him.

"I'm in love with you."

One evening, friends were visiting us. They had been caring

for their 101-year-old grandmother until her recent death. We were sharing some of our mutual experiences, and I told them of my role in the house and Grandma's confused love for my husband.

"And you feel jealous, don't you?" Terry confronted me, laughing. Our grandma did the same thing, and I felt that way."

"Isn't that absurd?" I asked as we both laughed at each other.

I guess the bonds of a good marriage run deeper than even we were aware.

At that point I remembered an incident that I couldn't help but share.

One fall afternoon Ed took Gram for a ride through the country, hoping to "bring her back." He talked about things in her past—places she had lived, her children.

"Remember Mine Hill, Gram? You lived there before you moved to Hackettstown."

"Oh, yes," she agreed.

"Remember your house in Stephensburg; all the beautiful flowers in your garden?"

After a long pause, she said, "Oh, yes, darling."

Ed felt somewhat content, as if maybe he had succeeded in triggering some memories. A few moments passed. She looked into his eyes.

"How long have we been married, anyway?"

We all laughed.

A recent change had occurred several days before. Gram sat in her chair. I sat on the couch nearby, and as had become his custom, Cody was sprawled out on the floor in front of Gram. She motioned to him. He sat up tall, perking his ears in expectation of a cookie or her dinner (if Gram didn't like something she would slip the plate in front of his nose, and he would quickly devour the evidence). I assumed it was loyalty that kept him there, but maybe it was more basic.

Grandma looked at him and quietly asked, "Would you get me a needle and thread?" Cody had such a bewildered expression on his face. He seemed to sense that this question was unusual. He just sat and stared at her.

Now, whether he liked it or not, Cody's role had changed as well. He had become a person.

THE UTTER FOLLY OF TAKING MATTERS INTO MY OWN HANDS

24

The heat of summer was upon us. The summer of 1994 was so frustrating to the family, as we were housebound. We were unable to leave Gram and Flip overnight; in fact, we had to be home by early evening to put Gram to bed. So even day trips were difficult. I was determined to do everything within my power to make the summer more pleasant, namely, convincing Ed that a pool might really solve the problem. In the past he would never consider it; he'd rather go to the river.

But now even that was no longer possible.

✠   ✠   ✠

FROM THE JOURNAL OF MARY WALSH
June 1995

Ed gave me the go-ahead to purchase a pool. It didn't matter that I knew nothing about above-ground pools. We were finally going to have a pool, and I felt up to the challenge.

Mistake number 1: Never send a novice to purchase an above-ground pool.

I shopped around and found the perfect pool. The price included installation. Ed thought it was too good to be true. (You know what they say.)

We decided on a sunny spot outside Gram and Flip's apartment. It was reasonably flat, or so I thought.

Friday the pool was to be installed. David was so excited!

Early Friday morning the installers arrived and proceeded to mark the spot by spraying a twenty-four-foot circle on the grass. We could almost envision it. Wow! Twenty-four feet was bigger than I thought; in fact, it was bigger than I wanted.

"Oh, Mrs. Walsh, I've got some bad news. This is solid rock. We can't dig even six inches."

I called Ed home from the office. The bad news was that we would need three dump truck loads of dirt—not just dirt, expensive select fill. The installer's price to bring in the dirt was two thousand dollars.

Ed was noticeably embarrassed as he took me aside.

"We'll have to send the pool back." David's countenance dropped considerably.

I felt terrible. My good intentions only frustrated him more.

✠   ✠   ✠

We did not send the pool back immediately, but let it sit in the boxes several days as we continued to roast in the sweltering heat. Ed had an idea. He had a customer who owed him money for a job he had estimated. He owned a dump truck and had access to free quarry dirt, not just dirt—select fill. They made a deal, and we had our dirt. Within a week Ed's customer had delivered two tandem truckloads of dirt to the pool location and began leveling it off. He planned to bring the final load the following Monday. It seemed safe to allow David to once again get excited.

I began calling around to find out who could come and fill the pool. I called a friend on the other side of the lake who had a pool installed last summer and she gave me the name of a farmer who would bring water at a reasonable price.

"Mary, did you get a permit?" she asked warily.

"No, I wasn't aware it was necessary for an above-ground pool."

"I hadn't gotten one either. My neighbor complained and we have to take our pool down. It's too close to my neighbors."

I assured her that the spot we had chosen was very secluded, no neighbors in sight except for an occasional bear in the wooded area nearby.

"I'll get one if it is required, but it's merely a technicality, I'm sure."

First thing the following morning I called the township zoning office and told the inspector I would be right down.

"I'm here for a pool permit."

"Where do you live?" he asked, not even glancing up at me.

"I live in Lake Valhalla."

"Oh, I'm sure you can't have a pool there. Most of the lots are small."

I sensed a negative approach.

"No, in fact our lot is one of the largest in the neighborhood. The location is far from any neighbor. I'm sure it won't be a problem."

"Your neighbor wants a pool and we've had a real hard time with him. Let me get my map."

He spread the map in front of me and without looking up pointed to our lot.

"Show me where you want to put the pool."

It took me a moment to figure out what I was looking at and where the actual spot was on the map.

"Here. Right on the side of the house. It's very secluded, sunny, not too far from the woods."

"You can't have a pool there; it has to be twenty feet from your neighbor's property line."

"The nearest home is at least one hundred feet away."

"No, the woods are your neighbor's."

I explained that the owners of the woods did not even live there.

"Sorry." He put his head down and went back to work. "You'd have to prove hardship," he said.

"Hardship? How about a family caring for two elderly ladies—one with advanced Alzheimer's, the other nearly blind—who can never leave their home for even a day?" I asked.

"Oh, no, *hardship* means you are unable to put the pool in any other location."

"How about two tandem-loads of dirt dumped in my backyard?"

He didn't even look up.

How will I ever tell Ed and David?

Lord, did I get ahead of you here? Was this all a terrible mistake? Please, forgive me if it was and work this out!

I cried and prayed all the way home.

I still was not prepared to break the news to David. I remembered where the owners of the woods lived. I drove there before going home and I explained my dilemma.

"I'd be more than happy to write a letter. I have no problem with you installing a pool near those woods." His wife stepped onto the porch and nodded her head in agreement.

I called the zoning office when I arrived home to report the encouraging news.

"Well, that will have to go before the board. The next meeting where it could be discussed won't be until late August. It'll cost you a hundred and fifty dollars to apply for the variance."

Ed and I agreed that we might go through all that and be turned down anyway. Was it worth it?

So now we had a pool in boxes sitting in the hot sun, and our formerly nice backyard full of dirt.

A few mornings later, I surveyed the yard for another not-so-perfect spot. I knew all the rules now—twenty feet from any property line, bears or no bears, at least ten feet from any sewer line. I spent the morning with a tape measure and suddenly realized there was another spot we could put the pool. It was not ideal, but if I could get it approved Ed agreed we would do it.

I made a trip to the courthouse and had a copy made of the

map of Lake Valhalla. I located our lot and the not-so perfect-spot
and drew a little circle representing the pool, lines clearly showing
all of the boundaries, and the fifteen feet between the pool and
sewer line. I drove directly to the inspector's office and laid it out
before him.

"That will be fine," he agreed as he wrote out a permit—without
looking up at me.

When I called the installer he said he would be able to move
the dirt from the perfect spot to the not-so-perfect-spot. He
would not be available, however, until the following week.

The days dragged by. David was counting.

"Only two more days, Mom!"

That evening I returned home from the store and parked Ed's
new car in its usual spot at the crest of the hill on the side of the
house. I was still getting used to driving a stick shift. It had been
many years, but it was coming back to me.

All the groceries put away, I sat down to talk to Ed.

"I have to run to the office. I'll just be a few minutes," he
assured me.

A few minutes—he wasn't kidding. The door opened suddenly,
and he stood before me looking as if he suspected I was playing a
trick on him. "Where is the Honda?" he asked.

"It's parked where we always park it!" I explained.

"It's not there," he assured me.

Jamie ran outside to investigate. The night was extremely dark
and still. It was an eerie feeling to realize the car was really gone.
My first thought was that it had been stolen.

"I promise you, I parked it right there!"

"Wait a minute, do you see something way down in the woods
over there?" Jamie said.

"I don't believe it. How did that happen?"

We followed the course the car had taken—down the hill,
across the spot where the pool was to be installed, and up and over
the ties that edged my garden. It had pulled out all my tomato
plants but left the row of marigolds unscathed. Traveling on into

the woods, it hit a tree and came to an abrupt stop, wedged between two trees.

I was so relieved after the car had been retrieved that no obvious damage had been done. Amazing.

But not nearly as relieved as when Ed and I simultaneously realized what could have happened. We looked at each other, and Ed said, "Thank the Lord the pool had not yet been installed!"

More amazing to me—after this night and the weeks of confusion due to my taking matters into my own hands—was that Ed could forgive me, and we could still laugh.

Thank you, Lord, for my husband!

☩   ☩   ☩

A more unusual marital strain developed as my and Ed's union gradually dissolved in Gram's mind. Although I could rationally stand back and realize that she had no control over this perception, the position it put me in was often an uncomfortable one. There was a time when Gram had been well aware that Ed and I were true-blue to each other—always had been, always would be— just as she and her husband had been. She took great delight in the closeness we shared. Yet she became very suspicious as the disease progressed.

One afternoon as I stood in the yard talking with the gentleman who lived next door, Gram became quite alarmed as she watched me from the kitchen window. It was the first time I had met our new neighbor.

"I'd keep an eye on that if I were you, Edward!" she warned him.

At other times she would whisper and tell me about the other woman Ed had upstairs. She was quite sure of it.

As I've shared previously, in her increasingly distorted world, Gram became the happily married wife of my husband. I personally felt more comfortable with their previous, grandmother/ grandson relationship. There were many comical incidents, yet those moments she perceived me as the intruder were very peculiar.

The most critical strain on our relationship throughout this experience was the painful question that would surface at times when I felt most overwhelmed: "At what point does your commitment to me, as your wife, take priority over the care of your grandmother?"

I hated the question. I wanted to care for her as long as possible, but at the points when I was weakest, that question would arise. The answers were not easy for Ed or myself.

Yes, Alzheimer's places a definite strain on even the closest of marriages.

✠   ✠   ✠

FROM THE JOURNAL OF MARY WALSH
October 1995
The final plunder of Gram's mind.

Something very sad has happened. I would think that after all I've witnessed with Gram's undoing, nothing would surprise me. But I was wrong.

I went downstairs yesterday morning to bathe Grandma. She sat counting, undisturbed by my presence. As I prepared to coax her from her chair, I noticed her silver wedding band on the floor beside her chair. I looked at her, remembering the many times she had announced that it had never—since the day she was married—been off her finger.

I was so taken back by the discovery that I wrote a poem.

THE SILVER RING
I found a ring today, a simple silver band,
Tossed carelessly beneath her feet
Now missing from her hand.
How oft' she'd grasp the slender ring
And bring to mind her special man,

Like no one else in all the world,
. . . . She'd not remove that silver band.
There could ne'er be another in her life,
So true a love, how deep her loss,
Yet for all the lonely days ahead,
She need only cast a glance, at that slender,
Precious silver ring,
. . . . How she loved that man.
I tried to slip the band back on
The restless hand that seemed so bare,
And remind her of her special love,
. . . . But there was no one there.
"Ninety-eight, ninety-nine,"
Her fingers busy counting,
As beloved memories, one by one,
Fall beneath her feet.
"One hundred"
Yet all that seems important is that
. . . . Her counting be complete.
But we remember for you, Gram,
The man you held so high,
And pass on this precious, silver band,
A token of the cherished love,
. . . . You thought could never die.

M. Walsh, October 1995

FROM THE JOURNAL OF MARY WALSH
January 1996—David's Wish

Grandma sits rather quietly now in her chair downstairs due to
medication and progression of the disease. In five short years, she
has regressed from an independent woman who delighted in

cradling great-grandchildren in her arms and bouncing toddlers on her knee, to one content to hold and talk to a lifeless, plastic doll. It is as if we have said a gradual good-bye. She is with us, but we miss her.

David recently asked me what I would wish if I could have any wish in the world—a favorite question of all young children. Before I could respond he said, "I would wish that Grandma could be like she used to be."

I wonder if that would have been my wish at eight years old.

RESPITE **25**

The word *respite* is to the mind of a caregiver what the word *oasis* is to a parched, weary desert traveler. Webster defines *respite* as temporary relief, as from work or pain. I had heard the word a number of times throughout our years of caring for Gram—always alluded to as something far-off and almost unattainable.

It brought to mind pleasant thoughts of relaxation—leisurely strolls along a white, sandy beach, collecting rare and beautiful shells as the sunlit waves rolled in and washed my bare feet. Having completed my collection—starfish, perhaps a sand dollar or two, an oyster with a rare pearl awaiting my discovery—I would find a blanket spread out beneath the golden rays of the midday sun inviting me to spend the rest of the day doing absolutely nothing! Perhaps I would begin a new chapter of my book while sipping a tall glass of iced tea.

After six years of caring for Gram, we were finally able to arrange a respite for the family.

As I look back to that fanciful ocean scene, I am amused. Why does a picture come to mind of a desert traveler, dying of thirst, skin blistered from the brutal sun, crawling with his last ounce of strength to reach that oasis—only to find that it was only a mirage?

The following is a journal entry relating some of the events of our long-awaited respite.

From the journal of Mary Walsh

October 1995

We are on vacation!

Not the Virgin Islands or even the Jersey Shore, but the Poconos—our own home!

We placed Gram in a nursing home for a one week "respite" and drove Flip to Liz's house in Delaware. The other day Ed and I were alone in our house for the first time since we moved here six years ago. I realize how much Alzheimer's afflicts us all; with the constant turmoil downstairs, an air of depression prevails. I have enjoyed being alone. I can't believe it will be over soon. I pray we can get Gram in a home soon. She has been on the list for a long time.

Ed took off from work Monday so we could take her to the home. It was a beautiful fall day. We had hoped to enjoy the ride home together, maybe stop at a farm stand, pick up some cider and fresh fruit. We took Ed's Honda (that poor car!). We realized about twenty minutes into the ride that the directions we were given were incorrect. All of a sudden, Gram started throwing up all over herself and the car. Flip had given her oatmeal and prune juice for breakfast. She threw up four times, smiling in between. I leaned into the backseat to try to help her. What a mess! Ed looked back at me in the rearview mirror. We both laughed. Gram did too.

Could it have happened any other way?

When we drove Flip to Delaware, we made a plan to stop at the shore before heading for home. Maybe we would sit on the sand for a while, talk, and unwind. We walked through the dunes to get to the beach, swatting ravenous flies and bugs. There had been a storm, and the waves churned up black dirt and deposited it all along the shore. In fact, the entire beach was black and covered with dead horseshoe crabs, hundreds of them, as far as the eye could see.

We took a picture to remember our outing.

✠   ✠   ✠

Not long after our respite, the hospice was replaced by another nursing service, so we no longer saw our nurse, Laura. One day as I was leaving the office, I ran into her. We hugged, and she told me she had just come from the dentist.

"I'm going to lose all my teeth within the next few months," she said with a sigh.

Her dentist had discovered in her x-rays a disease of the jaw-bone, most likely from her cancer treatments. It would result in all her teeth loosening and falling out.

"One of my front teeth fell out this morning."

"I'm sorry. I didn't notice any tooth missing."

"I used Super Glue to put it back so I could go to work. My dentist couldn't believe it," she said, laughing.

I marveled at her ingenuity and devotion to work. "You're too much."

We shared amazement at the seemingly endless onslaught of life's trials.

"They will have an end someday, won't they?" I asked.

"It's looking better all the time," she concluded.

I Wish You Hadn't Asked That   26

"Mommy, if you had to pick, would you rather be very rich or very famous?" David asked me with a faraway look of little-boy wonder.

"Well, Dave, I guess if I were to choose, I would have to say rich. After all, there are many ways a person might become famous. Maybe rich is a safer choice."

There is a thin line between famous and infamous. A person reveling in popularity today could be headline news on the scandal sheets tomorrow, maybe through little fault of his own. Why, even an ordinary Pocono housewife simply going about her usual daily routine might find herself thrust into the limelight and wonder, *Will my life ever be normal again?* or worse yet, come to realize, that perhaps this *is* "normal."

I hesitate to tell this story, yet how can I not relate the most unbelievable turn of events that came into my life in the midst of caring for Grandma.

FROM THE JOURNAL OF MARY WALSH
January 1995
If I did not have the newspaper article to prove it, one would think I made this up.

It is so incredible.

*It seems to be the most terrible thing that could have
happened, and it all began with a question.*

✛   ✛   ✛

Seven-year-old Jamie awaited the arrival of my twins. He watched
the sacrifice of many to keep me off my feet. He heard the prayers
for their survival. Would they be boys or girls? He did not know,
but he anxiously awaited the day of their birth. And then at
twenty-six weeks, after their premature birth and death, he stood
at their graveside. He felt the loss as we all did. He was keenly
aware that we did not "dispose" of their bodies. They were buried
in the cemetery—given the same treatment as any other persons.

He learned early in his life that even at their earliest stages of
development, babies are human beings.

One evening while he was in high school, I sat watching a
documentary on the holocaust—the slaughter of millions of innocent Jewish people. Tears streamed down my cheeks as I viewed in
disbelief the skeletal bodies being bulldozed into an open grave. It
had not been the first time I had seen these films, yet my reaction
was always the same.

"Why are you crying, Mom?" Jamie asked as he passed through
the room.

I sensed it to be one of those questions.

"It's just so unbelievable, Jamie."

"Mom, don't you realize it is no different than what is taking
place right now with the slaughter of millions of helpless babies?"

From his earliest years, Jamie had a history of asking the
deepest, most probing questions. At age six he was so enamored
with Ed's computer work that he sat down and had Ed begin to
teach him. Within a few years, Ed was no longer able to answer his
computer-related questions. He had to find things out for himself.
He went on to master it, and by age of twenty-three, he managed
the technical and trading aspects of a NASDAQ electronic trading
floor on Wall Street. Forty traders rely on him to keep things
running smoothly.

At age thirteen, a series of questions opened up an interest in astronomy that continued through high school. He read all the books on the subject he could get his hands on. He graduated from a telescope that we gave him for his thirteenth birthday to a secondhand, eight-inch refractor that he purchased on his own. He spent countless, starry nights outside—observing and sharing with anyone interested. On a number of occasions I found myself trying to keep warm in the wee hours of the morning at a local observatory, listening to him converse with other adult astronomers at a level that was quite astounding.

He had mastered the subject because he wanted to know all he could about it.

The following is an excerpt from his diary about the greatest gift he had ever received:

> The greatest physical gift I ever received, other than my life that is, was my telescope. Few people can appreciate the marvelous wonders one can behold with such a gift. Since I received it last July I have seen the glorious rings of Saturn, the planets Venus, Mars, and Jupiter. I have stared in awe at the veritable treasury of craters and the like on the moon. I have located the Andromeda Galaxy, the globular cluster M13 in Hercules, and the double open cluster in Perseus. Besides that, my telescope sparked a lifelong interest.
>
> So far I have learned more on one subject than I have ever before.

At an early age, Jamie displayed a love for and understanding of God's Word far beyond his tender years. It was, however, more than just a head knowledge. I would often overhear him singing psalms from the Bible and praying, especially that his little brother Christopher "would learn to obey Mommy and Daddy." I would find poems he had written as the one that follows.

MY WONDERFUL GOD
All rivers must flow
All living things grow
All stars must shine

And the moon must glow.
But is this by work divine
Or just by chance, who can know?
I can.
My God is wonderful and great
   The director of all the world's fate.
He controls the seasons
And all events for his own reasons.
In the beginning God created all things
   What shame to God man's foolish philosophy of evolution
      brings
   The God who all things makes.
While the carnal man mocks God's awesome power,
   The righteous man awakes.

Jamie Walsh, fourth grade

It was both a surprise and disappointment to us in ninth grade when we realized he was "straddling the fence." In tenth grade he jumped headlong to the other side, but by eleventh grade he was on the fence again, beginning to see that he must take a side. He participated in many creation versus evolution debates. He had studied both subjects extensively through the years and was well equipped. He was involved in many discussions about abortion—a very troubling subject to Jamie.

At the start of his senior year, Jamie expressed a desire to be home schooled. He felt strongly that he could not sit another year under teaching so contrary to everything he believed. He enrolled in a home school program that would grant him credits for his work, and since I obviously could not teach him, he enrolled in courses at the local college. Since he was always a self-motivated learner, he had a great year.

Halfway through the year he began asking a question. It was definitely one of those questions. He posed it as follows:

"Do Christians have the right and/or responsibility to use deadly force in the defense of the unborn?"

My reaction, typical of most, was "Of course not, Jamie, that would be murder; two wrongs don't make a right." End of question.

"What if those babies were three-year-olds, and they were being taken in to be murdered? What would my obligation be? Just stand there? What really is the difference?"

Growing up in a day when it is legal to take the life of your child while it is concealed within the womb yet face murder charges if you take that same life seconds after it is born, causes distress to anyone with common sense and an understanding of God's law.

✠   ✠   ✠

Realizing this question was very important to Jamie, I gave it a lot of thought. I tried to imagine an abortion clinic in my own neighborhood. How would I react if I knew for a fact that the women walking through that door were there to have their babies killed?

What if they were three-year-olds?

Would I simply drive by day after day? I remembered my surprising reaction to my children being saluted in the name of Hitler at the roller rink.

These were hard questions to think about.

Meanwhile, Jamie continued to ask the question of pastors and other adult friends he respected. His question evolved into a paper in which he thoroughly explored the subject. He always made it clear that he had not concluded his question to be right, but that it was something he had to settle in his own mind.

He would cite a scripture such as Proverbs 24:11-12 (NIV):

RESCUE THOSE BEING LED AWAY TO DEATH; HOLD BACK THOSE STAGGERING TOWARD SLAUGHTER. IF YOU SAY, "BUT WE KNEW NOTHING ABOUT THIS," DOES NOT HE WHO WEIGHS THE HEART PERCEIVE IT? DOES NOT HE WHO GUARDS YOUR LIFE KNOW IT? WILL HE NOT REPAY EACH PERSON ACCORDING TO WHAT HE HAS DONE?

Ed knew as well as I did that this question was just not going to go away.

Then something happened that intensified the situation.

"Mom, did you hear the news?" Jamie asked over the phone while I was at the office one day.

"No, Jamie, what?"

"There was a shooting at an abortion clinic in Florida, and listen to this: the man who did the shooting is a former pastor in our denomination."

A chill went through me.

I knew this would have a profound impact on my son. He had high regard for the elders and pastors in our denomination, seeing them as noble and honorable men. He even went so far as to call the pastor, Paul Hill, in prison, telling him of the paper he had written and the turmoil he was in. He desperately wanted to settle this question in his mind.

It was a very strange and unnerving time.

Jamie was not the only person affected by these events. Little did I realize that it was having a tremendous impact on Ed. Although he did not support Paul Hill's action and told him so, he wanted him to have the right to a defensive action trial and therefore signed a petition to that effect.

We also found that Jamie was not the only one asking questions. Literature circulated concerning the issue, and there were discussions taking place all over the Internet. Because congregations were in turmoil, a number of reputable churches were holding debates to discuss the issue. They realized it must not be ignored, but settled.

Ed accompanied Jamie to several debates.

✠   ✠   ✠

FROM THE JOURNAL OF MARY WALSH
August 1995

When I wake up in the morning, I forget for a moment all that is going on around me. Then I remember. I feel sickened. I wish it would go away, but it does not.

It is hard to believe that Grandma's diaper changes have become the easy part of my life.

✠ ✠ ✠

One afternoon we received a letter from Karen Hill, Paul Hill's wife, a Christian and mother of three small children. Although I did not support her husband's action, I got down on my knees, letter in hand and cried out to the Lord. *We need a resolution. This is tearing us apart. Please help us.*

There are times when things are so beyond our own power that we cry out in utter weakness to the Lord—and the despair is replaced by an unexpected peace and faith that the outcome is safely in his hands. This was one of those times. Within half an hour I received a call from a pastor friend in New York. He asked to speak to Jamie. I prayed.

The Lord used this man in a special way that day, helping to settle this issue once and for all. Jamie assured him that he would consider seriously what they had discussed. Immediately upon hanging up, he called his father and told him about the conversation. Between the two of them, Jamie's questions were answered.

It was as if a heavy weight had been lifted from all of us. The issue of abortion will never be put to rest as long as they are taking place; but this particular question was no longer discussed in our home.

Several months later we heard on the news that there was another shooting at an abortion clinic in Massachusetts. This time several workers at the clinic were also shot. There was talk that the individual who did the shooting was a very troubled, mentally unstable individual. Naturally this was big news, the issue of abortion being the most impassioned one in our country.

"Mary, I got a call from a reporter from the *Philadelphia Inquirer*. She wants to do an interview," Ed told me.

"An interview for what?" I asked.

"She wants to know more about the Defensive Action Movement because of the shooting in Massachusetts. She contacted me because I had signed that petition months ago."

"And you said no, right?"

"I told her that I do not support that action, and that she would be wasting her time driving here. She said she wanted to interview me, anyway, as one who understood the thinking behind it."

"And you said no, right?"

"I really think it will be an opportunity to speak out against abortion. I said OK."

"Ed, do you have any idea what she could do to you? This is the media!"

"She'll be at our house tonight at eight. I just feel I have to do what I can. I may never have this opportunity to speak out again."

I did not want to be present at the interview. Then I realized I needed to be there to witness what was being said.

The interviewer was very friendly, commenting on our home and admiring Gram's seaport painting. Jamie wanted to be involved in the interview also. I was on the edge of my seat.

I said only one thing. "I want you to know that this family has been through a lot these past months because of this question. It has been settled that the violence is wrong. I want to make that fact very clear. I do not want any misunderstandings about this."

As we got into the discussion, having made it very clear that we did not support these shootings, I began to relax a bit.

The discussion shifted to our views of abortion. Jamie shared his belief that there is no difference between a baby in the womb—at any stage of development—and a three-year-old.

Before leaving, the reporter had one last request. Could she take our picture?

"You're such a nice-looking family. It would be great for the article."

Ed hesitated. I looked at him shaking my head no. I felt ill at ease.

Even before I woke up Sunday morning, I felt anxious. Ed had run out for the newspaper assuming the article would be in it.

It was—on the very front page!

Ed read the opening sentence and I honestly believed he was joking.

He was not.

The headline read, in bold letters, "Abortion Fight's Lethal Side."

"In a Pocono living room with afghans on the couch and a seaport painting on the wall, Edward Walsh III and his teenage son explain why shooting people at abortion clinics is a good idea."

I have rarely hit the ceiling, but I did that day.

The article covered almost two full pages and intimated that Ed and Jamie were spokesmen for the movement. They were included among all those who had previously been involved in abortion clinic shootings. There was absolutely no distinction made between them and us.

How thankful I was that we had said no to the picture.

I was afraid to go out of the house. There seemed to be more cars than usual passing by. Jamie received a death threat over the phone the first day.

A talk radio show opened with the host reading the following:

"In a Pocono living room with afghans on the couch and a seaport painting on the wall, Edward Walsh III and his teenage son explain why shooting people at abortion clinics is a good idea."

It was followed by another statement: "Perhaps it is time for us to exercise our right to free speech and call for the shooting of animals like this."

Ed drove directly home, pulled into the driveway, and ran into the house.

"I've got to use the phone!" He was shaking noticeably.

"What's the matter?"

"I've got to get through," he said, pushing buttons frantically.

He was put on the air and attempted to explain what had happened.

"This is Edward Walsh, and I want to make it clear that I do not believe shooting people at abortion clinics is a good idea. I was grossly misquoted and misrepresented."

He emphasized the fact that he was very opposed to abortion but did not support that action.

Ed received calls from several major television stations wanting him to appear on various news shows. He declined.

We contacted the paper the following day, expressing our outrage. From that call we learned that the article would appear in possibly three hundred papers around the country. And if that wasn't enough, Ed received a call from a friend in Michigan whose pastor had read the story on the Internet.

There just wasn't a pillow big enough to hide my head under.

The paper agreed to print a retraction. It appeared as a tiny two-inch statement on the second page the following day. Somehow I doubt it made the same impact as the first article.

Ed and I were devastated by the incident. He had a lot of explaining to do. The presbytery of our denomination called immediately. He apologized to them, as he did to me and our church and anyone else affected, for his terrible indiscretion in granting the interview and for all the hurt it had caused.

Saying I'm sorry did not defuse the anger and humiliation that would follow. Expecting support, rebuke and further humiliation followed.

The following Monday morning I was attempting to get things in perspective. Ed had gone to work. I was standing at the sink doing dishes, thinking about all that had happened. I noticed two well-dressed men walking toward the door.

I was not in the mood to be proselytized.

It was just the FBI.

"Gee, I wonder why you are here!" I laughed nervously as I let them inside. I picked up the phone.

"Ed, we have some visitors. I think you should come home."

"This isn't exactly what we expected," the FBI agent said, looking around our home, perhaps to reassure me.

They couldn't have been more personable. After we explained what had happened, and having had personal experience with the tactics of the media, they turned their attention toward our protection. They had some real concerns. We were given all their phone numbers and told to call at anytime, day or night.

When I finally ventured out to the food store, I noticed a few cashiers' heads turning. Neighbors had read the article. It was extremely uncomfortable.

After the smoke had cleared, we began attending a nearby church. We wanted to get more involved with people in the area, realizing after all we had been through that we needed the support of friends. When it came down to actually joining, six months later, Ed was told they were "afraid of him" because of the article. We could have stayed and tried to work through things, but at that point there wasn't anything left in us. We were physically and emotionally spent.

As I write this two years later, we continue to feel the effects of that article. I have witnessed firsthand the damage the media can do to a reputation. I see that it is nearly impossible to remedy a damaged reputation. That loss can have a crushing effect on the spirit of a person.

I've observed how others rally at the loss of a home to fire or a loved one to the grave, but working through the loss of a reputation has taken us down a very lonely path.

✠   ✠   ✠

I've discovered there's always a bit of humor to be found, though, even at the darkest of times. One day, realizing the extent of the damage that had been done, Ed threw up his hands half joking and said to David, "The whole world's against me, David!"

David tried to comfort him, "Oh, Dad, it's only this country!"

✠   ✠   ✠

FROM THE JOURNAL OF MARY WALSH
December 1996

It's Sunday morning, and I'm on Grandma duty. The rest of the family is in church.

Grandma is seated in her chair, strapped in, with a doll cradled in her arms. She looks into its eyes every few minutes and smiles.

"Hi! I'm your mother! You're happy aren't you? Say you're happy. Say 'I'm happy.' "

Now she's telling me she's "going." That means I'm in trouble, because she will soon insist on getting out of her chair to go.

"We love you. Do you love us?"

This morning I bathed and dressed her and tried to get her to her chair. She forced her way over to the dresser and picked up a bobby pin and looked at it as if she had found a fine jewel. She clipped it onto her earlobe. Then she picked up a barrette and tried to clip it onto her other earlobe. She would have hurt her ear if I hadn't stopped her. We walked to her chair. She was so proud of her earring that I had to call Dawn down to see it. Grandma assured Dawn she could have a pair also.

We are so used to these bizarre incidents that we often don't even comment on them.

THE LAST STRAW | 27

FROM THE JOURNAL OF MARY WALSH
September 1995

I shut off the vacuum cleaner and ran to the door. Cody had been barking as he did when any deliveryman set foot on the property. It was comical to see the UPS man cower inside his truck until I called him inside. Great watchdog!

If they only knew how harmless he really is.

The mailman had pulled up the driveway.

"He must have a package," I thought. No, in fact it was a registered letter, very official looking. I signed for it and walked toward the house as I read over the unfamiliar return address. It was obviously from a law firm.

"What in the world could this be?"

I tore open the envelope and removed a very official stack of papers, at least ten sheets. I read over the first page. It was so unbelievable that it took a second reading for it to sink in. I picked up the phone and dialed Ed's office.

"Ed, are you sitting down?" I asked.

"What's wrong, hon?"

"I just signed for a registered letter. It appears that you and Walsh Estimating Service are being sued for 'conspiring to commit fraud.'" I then read him the first page. This was serious. I thought of that scripture from James:

CONSIDER IT PURE JOY, MY BROTHERS, WHENEVER YOU FACE TRIALS OF MANY KINDS, BECAUSE YOU KNOW THAT THE TESTING OF YOUR FAITH DEVELOPS PERSEVERANCE. JAMES 1:2-3, NIV

✠   ✠   ✠

We certainly had faced trials of many kinds. There was something very different, however, about this latest and very threatening potential trial. After studying the charges, getting through all the legal jargon, and finally realizing who this person was and what had happened, we believed it to be a frivolous and absolutely outrageous accusation. More than that, we saw it as a terrible intrusion—the "last straw" if you will. It was the last thing we needed.

To be brief, years earlier Ed met a gentleman who owned a large farm. He was hoping to sell a portion of it, or develop it himself. He hired Ed to do a budget estimate to see what the cost would be to develop the property. Ed never visited the site, as he might for a more thorough estimate, but worked up some preliminary costs. Years later, the property was sold, and Ed's name and business were included in the contract without Ed's knowledge. The buyer used Ed's by then outdated and low-cost figures to secure a bank loan and began to develop the property. He lost a great deal of money on the project. The only way he could have the contract reversed was to prove there had been a "conspiracy to commit fraud" between the seller and Ed. Even though Ed had not worked with the buyer directly in these negotiations, Ed was being sued.

My immediate response, realizing all Ed had been through with the scandalous newspaper article and his already disheartened frame of mind, was to try to put a stop to this. I wrote a very personal letter to this man, sharing with him some of the very hard times we had been through, about Ed's grandmother, and our years of heartache with our son. I shared with him the fact that Ed was an honest man, a Christian, had built his business dealing honestly with all of his customers, and that these allegations were ridiculously out of character for such a man. I pleaded with him to give us a break and not drag us through this.

My letter was ineffective. We continued to get letters from his lawyer.

We sought council from a lawyer and came away discouraged. If we fought this, we could expect to pay at least $50,000 in legal fees. If we were to lose the case, we would lose all we had worked for the past eight years, plus the $50,000. If we were to win, it would only cost us the $50,000 for the lawyer. Either way we would likely be forced into bankruptcy.

The two options were not very appealing. We decided on a third.

"I do not have $50,000 to give to a lawyer. That's like buying something I can't afford," Ed concluded.

"It would be one thing if you were guilty, but you're innocent! What a terrible waste of money we don't have," I added.

"Mary, I wish I was guilty, because I'd show them—I'd be the first one to admit it."

I knew this to be true of my husband.

✠   ✠   ✠

After visiting several lawyers at $180 per hour, we saw how quickly $2,000 disappeared. Ed decided he really did not have a choice. He would have to defend himself without a lawyer. It was a scary thought. I worried that Ed would not be able to handle this added stress.

I soon realized that I could not continue our trips to lawyers' offices and court and also care for Gram round the clock.

"Why haven't we heard from the nursing home yet?" Ed asked.

"She's been on the list for ten months; I don't know why I haven't heard. Six months ago they thought it would be soon."

I called and spoke with the woman in charge of admissions.

"Laura Walsh is not on the list," she assured me.

"There must be some mistake. She was put on ten months ago, and six months ago I was told it should be soon."

"My understanding is that there was 'a question about her finances' according to the state. She lost her place and is no longer on the list."

My heart sank.

"I don't understand. The welfare office told me ten months ago that everything was in order and it was just a matter of waiting for an opening. We are in a real crisis here."

"There are cases where we can make an exception if it is obvious there is real hardship. Meanwhile, call the welfare office and see what they say."

I hung up the phone and called the welfare office. I asked to speak with the woman who had assured me everything was in order ten months earlier.

"Well, we had a question about the sale of your grandmother's house."

"Yes, we discussed that in your office. I told you the house was sold seven years ago, well before your look-back period. We concluded that it had nothing to do with the case, and you assured me she was on the list and would be admitted as soon as there was an opening."

"Well, it has been longer than 120 days, you'll have to send me a copy of the contract that proves the date of the sale—and then reapply."

"Reapply? And wait another ten months? I will gladly send you that information, but why didn't you ask me for this ten months ago? Ten months is a long time when you're changing diapers and caring for someone around the clock."

I got off the phone, noticeably upset. It was obvious someone had not done her job.

"Hon, you should never assume that someone has done their job, especially in an office like that. Unless you keep on top of those things, they don't happen," Ed reminded me.

I had not given up on the effectiveness of letter writing. I still believed I was dealing with human beings—if I could just make them see the need here. I sat down and composed a letter to the woman in charge of admissions at the nursing home. I shared some of what we had undergone during the seven years caring for Gram and concluded with the pending litigation and my need to support my husband at this time.

Within three days Gram was admitted.

I believe my letter was effective.

Ed believes it had something to do with a notation at the end of the letter indicating that copies were sent to several doctors, the admissions director at the nursing home, the Office of Aging, and the Deputy Secretary for Medical Assistance for the state of Pennsylvania.

Either way, she was in.

FROM THE JOURNAL OF MARY WALSH
September 1996

The lawsuit has been ongoing for a year. It's taking a heavy toll on Ed. He rarely sleeps through a night; I wake up to find he is gone. I wake up and pray for him. I'm sure he was awakened once to do something in regard to the lawsuit. Or is it simply in torment that this false accusation robs so much from his health, business, and finances?

I have reflected on the wonderful things about my husband. I think back to our "new beginning," our marriage, how Ed, with no encouragement from his parents went to work—rarely missing a day in all our married life. To each job he gave his best, always moving ahead. He started as a janitor on a construction site, to foreman, to construction estimator—on to vice president of several construction companies. He has always been a diligent and reliable worker.

I recall the occasions when he left potentially promising positions because of dishonesty on the part of an employer—offering to pay him "under the table" or dealing dishonestly with clients. It was because of this that Walsh Estimating came into existence. He wanted to run a business honorably.

Now to have the humiliation of being accused of conspiring to commit fraud. It is so contrary to all his life has stood for. His pain over this breaks my heart. But at the same time, I'm filled with praise and admiration for this man.

I love him dearly.

IN HER ELEMENT

"Just put her in a nursing home."

Many people offered that advice to me—especially during the difficult years of Gram's illness—but our promise to Gram years earlier postponed our decision. When the time finally came, we were pleasantly surprised at Gram's immediate adjustment to her new surroundings. There were no feelings of guilt to grapple with—we could see clearly that she was actually better off than she was at home. Of course, the particular home she was in had everything to do with our and her satisfaction.

"Mom, we have to get Grandma up and walk her," David would often remind me during her final months at home. "She might forget how if we don't!"

We did walk her through the halls, even outside at times. Often she did not want to get up, so she sat most of the day. During her first week in the nursing home she was seated in a wheelchair and quickly learned to "walk" herself around the halls. This opened up a whole new world to her. She was able to go anywhere on the floor, unrestricted. There was so much to see. She made friends quickly, sharing her "numbers" with all she met. Some of the patients stared blankly at her, others counted along with her.

"One, two, three, four, five," she'd count, extending her hand to a gentleman in a wheelchair.

"Give me five!" he'd reply, assuming that to be her intent. She'd give him more than five: "Six, seven, eight, nine, ten," she'd continue, smiling.

Within a few weeks they had her on her feet, walking through the halls. We could always identify her still graceful posture, hand often casually in a pocket or on one hip, moving through the halls as if she owned the place. If we couldn't find her right away, we would look around and often discover her in someone's room or having lunch with the nurses in their lunchroom. They liked her company. Although she was unable to say much more than an occasional word (aside from the numbers), her smile was magnetic, and she freely shared it with all she encountered. In fact, everyone loved Laura.

The other patients on the floor were in much the same condition as Gram. It was an emotional time, but we would always find humor to lighten the heaviness. One of Gram's new friends had to be redressed every few minutes; she insisted on taking everything off from the waist up. Then there was Vera, a boisterous, large woman, full of off-color jokes. She was hard as nails. I was often relieved she couldn't remember the punch lines. When she did, she'd laugh so hard she'd make Grandma laugh. If only Gram knew what she was laughing at. They would often sit together, holding hands. They were a most unlikely pair.

On Saturday mornings, the entire lunchroom was filled with patients glued to the television, watching Saturday morning cartoons. They seemed content, but it was a sad picture. Gram was no longer interested in television at all.

FROM THE JOURNAL OF MARY WALSH
February 1996

I'm finding myself in somewhat a state of mourning, not for the grandma we took to the nursing home, but for Laura Walsh, the energetic, positive thinking dynamo.

When I stopped at the nursing home to pick Flip up yesterday, we were told there would be a "flower show" in the activity room. We pushed Gram in her wheelchair to the room. She is all over the halls in her chair! Other residents in their wheelchairs surrounded the table. I surveyed the room—some had their mouths open, eyes closed; some their heads hanging down. Grandma sat counting to one hundred. I had to wonder how much of the flower show they were going to take in.

As we turned to leave, I'm sure Flip felt as I did. It was as if we realized Gram was finally at the point where we could turn and leave. She was much like the others. There was no more fight. She no longer struggled to hang on to her reality. She is gone, and I often find myself in tears for her.

FROM THE JOURNAL OF MARY WALSH
March 1996

Wonderful things are happening!

This is a little premature, yet I'm so excited I want to record it.

We've noticed some real changes in Chris over the past months. As Dawn has moved into that difficult, nearly impossible stage, he has been advising me as to how I should deal with her.

He said to her one night, "Remember, Dawn, Mom and Dad haven't changed, it's you who is changing."

Then he told us he hoped to go to Arizona with a mission group this summer.

I noticed my old Bible and other books, such as, How to Be Sure You Are a Christian next to his bed. I've also noticed the radio has been tuned to a Christian station after he has driven the car.

One morning I was wakened at four o'clock. I felt an unusual rush of excitement and prayed for him. I couldn't sleep. I got up and realized his light was on. He said he couldn't sleep. I had the wonderful feeling that the Lord was working in his heart in some way.

The other night he asked Ed if he could talk to him privately. Ed closed the door, wondering if he would break some bad news to him, prepared for the worst. They were in there for a long time. I wondered what was going on. When they finally opened the door, they came out smiling, but it was obvious they had both been crying.

Later Ed told me Chris had said to him, "Dad, I want you to know that I believe everything you ever taught me." He cried and apologized for all he had put us through and said he wanted to follow Christ. They talked at length. Ed said, "You had better go tell your mother what you told me."

Chris took me in his room, shut the door, and sat me down. He hugged me as never before and in tears told me how sorry he was for all he had put me through. Naturally, I cried. He told me also of his desire to follow Christ. He struggles for assurance, wondering at times if he had gone too far. It's exciting.

FROM THE JOURNAL OF MARY WALSH
May 1996

Three months passed with little change. One day in early May we were disturbed by the fact that Gram seemed totally unaware that we were visiting her. She stared blankly in front of her and did not respond to our attempts to talk to her. Usually we could get her to smile, but something had changed. There had been a flu circulating through the nursing home, and we wondered if she was coming down with it, though she had no fever or obvious symptoms.

Two days later a nurse called to tell us that she was in bed and seemed to want to stay there. Flip and I drove right over and spent

*the morning with her, though she seemed totally unaware of our
presence. We held her hands and prayed for her, aware that she
could possibly still hear us. As I sat holding her hands, I couldn't
help but admire them once again, those lovely, graceful hands.*

*"These hands have given so much, haven't they, Flip? Think
of all the knitting they've done, the pie crusts they've rolled—all
the comfort they've given."*

We were both aware that she would not be with us much longer.

"I'd like to stay for the afternoon," Flip said quietly.

*Ed arrived to pick her up before dinner and spent some time
before leaving for home. As they were leaving, Ed's sister Sharon
arrived and stayed for a while.*

✠   ✠   ✠

Ed and Flip stepped out into the fading sunlight and walked
silently to the car. Aware of how distraught she was, Ed assured
Flip that I would return with her first thing in the morning.

That evening around seven-thirty, the phone rang.

"Mrs. Walsh, this is Irene from the nursing home."

I thought she might tell us to rush right over.

"I'm afraid I have some bad news. Laura Walsh passed away at
six forty-five, not long after her granddaughter left for home. I
want you to know that she died very peacefully."

I was alone in the room and stood quietly holding the phone,
tears welling up for this woman. An image of Gram before Alzheimer's filled my mind—that elegant posture, that vivacious smile,
the outstretched hands that could never do enough for us. Then I
thought of the pitiful, frail image Flip and I prayed over that
morning and burst into tears. I prayed that I would know how to
break the news to Flip. Surely, if we had known death was imminent, we would have stayed. But we thought it was weeks away.

I walked downstairs where Flip sat quietly. I walked over and
hugged her. She seemed like a frail little bird. I hated to tell her.

"Oh, Gramma, Gramma, Gramma . . ." she cried. "She suffered so much, Mary."

She sat there worn out from years of caring for her sister, her older sister who had become more like a baby. She cried deeply for Gram, this woman who had been her lifelong friend and companion.

As each of our children heard the news, they went down to comfort Flip.

We each had our own time of grieving for Gram, reminiscing about the things that so endeared her to us. For years, she had been more like a mother to Ed than a grandmother.

My heart yearned for the woman who became more of a friend to me than a mother-in-law—one who inspired me in so many ways, simply by her example. There could never be a value placed on our children's experience—spending so much time with a great-grandmother so spry and excited about life. Yes, we would all miss our Grandma Walsh.

FROM THE JOURNAL OF MARY WALSH
May 1996

Of all the children, David seems to be taking Gram's death the hardest. Although he knew little of his healthy, independent grandmother (only the confused, tormented woman who depended on others for even her most basic needs), her helplessness has wrought in him a compassionate spirit I believe he will have throughout his life. He cried deeply for her.

☩   ☩   ☩

Ed and I hugged each other, realizing we both felt a strange sense of relief. We did not go through the gut-wrenching grieving that accompanies many deaths. That had been spread out over the years as we witnessed her regression from one stage to the next. The greatest relief of all was realizing the gross indignities of this insidious disease were now behind Gram.

There had been several years when we hesitated to have company over at all because we never knew how Gram would behave. One year, I made the bold decision to invite several couples over for dinner on Ed's birthday. We made it clear to Flip that she should call us if she needed help. Dinner was ready—Ed's favorite—eggplant parmesan. As I walked to the front door to let our friends in, Flip called frantically from downstairs. Ed let the guests in, and I ran down. Flip was in the bathroom with Gram, and the sight was pitiful. Just as a toddler might do, she had taken her diaper off and covered her body with the contents. It was not only all over her body; it was everywhere.

We managed to get her into the tub, though she was not a willing participant. We bathed her completely, washed her hair and got her to bed. Then, of course, we scrubbed the entire bathroom.

By the time I got upstairs and had washed and changed my clothes, the "happy" in happy birthday had all but disappeared. Of course I didn't tell our friends what the delay had been—I didn't think it would be appropriate before dinner. As for me, I let the eggplant pass me right by.

Gut-wrenching experiences such as this, along with the numerous indignities she suffered, were the reason for the great relief Ed and I felt on Gram's behalf when she died. How many times had we gone downstairs to find her totally disrobed except for a sock. Yes, we were saddened but relieved for her.

We protected our children from as much of it as we could, but at times they were shocked as well. I remember one day while the children were watching TV, Gram came in and with great delight tried to hand one of them something she had found in the kitty litter box.

These are stories I rarely tell, wondering at times if I should at all. They are taken from a chapter that will never be written. Yet the Alzheimer's nightmare is not complete without them. It is why the grieving process is so very different.

I am sure that any family caring for an Alzheimer's victim will understand what I am saying. There were incidents Ed and I witnessed that we could never share with anyone, and our hearts broke for her when they occurred. It is because of the demoralizing events of this unwritten chapter that our mourning was the most unusual. We all shed tears, but most of our grieving had been done throughout the previous seven years. We were so saddened, yet truly relieved for our grandmother. The indignities of this disease are almost beyond my ability to describe them.

I do look forward to seeing her again one day. We all do. The image of Gram in heaven, fully restored, is a wonderful thought to us. I can just see her radiant smile moving gracefully among the angels. She probably tends the most beautiful garden imaginable—without a weed in it.

And I'll just bet she's waiting with those outstretched arms as she always did—waiting to say "Enter, family!"

✠   ✠   ✠

FROM THE JOURNAL OF MARY WALSH
August 1997

The O. J. Simpson case has come and gone and is old news now. Our litigation, however, drags on and may continue into the next year. It has been two long years already. The long days of depositions are so hard on Ed. The plaintiff is so hateful toward him, calling him a liar and an unethical businessman. It is difficult to remain silent as he falsely accuses my husband—but I have. We see the effect on our business. Ed figures we have probably lost at least $20,000 due to our involvement, actual money spent and loss of productivity—and that is without the cost of a lawyer.

We received a package in the mail today from the plaintiff's attorney. We had not been made aware until now what this man really wants as a result of the lawsuit. He is hoping to receive $3,200,000 (yes, that's millions) from the two "conspirators." When Ed told me, we hugged each other and burst out laughing.

"How do we get in these outrageous situations?" he asked.

I should have faith in our legal system, and I pray that the truth will prevail.

I will, however, trust the Lord. His truth will prevail. Not necessarily in this life, but ultimately. That I know for sure.

𝒥t was one of those early spring mornings that could fill even the faintest of hearts with hope—bursting with promise and new life—a clear blue sky and birds on the wing rejoicing in the crisp spring air. This would be a very different funeral.

When asked by the funeral director if we had a minister we would like for him to contact, Ed and I looked at each other. For the first time in many years, we did not.

"I have a list of ministers. I can pick one for you if you like," he had offered.

No, we did not want a stranger. That would be too impersonal. As difficult as it would be, Ed decided he would handle it himself.

"Have you given any thought to flowers? Perhaps you would like to select some from our catalog?"

He opened the catalog and placed it in front of us. The pages depicted traditional arrangements of deep, purplish-red roses and white carnations—funeral bouquets.

I pictured her spring gardens, bursting with red and yellow tulips and daffodils.

"Thank you, but I think I'd like to take care of that myself," I told the gentleman.

"I would like simple bouquets, as if they had been picked right from her garden," I explained to the florist later that afternoon, "Tulips, daffodils, daisies—spring flowers!"

And now, as her grandchildren and great-grandchildren were placing the flowers on Gram's casket, so fresh and beautifully simple, I couldn't help but realize how important these things were to her—her family and her joy in giving them pleasure through her labors.

Before beginning the service, Ed asked me to read a tribute I had written, entitled "Grandma's Garden." Quickly realizing I could not get through it, Jamie took over.

Anyone who knew Grandma Walsh has a memory of her on her knees in the dirt digging deep into the earth to plant something we would all enjoy the following season. It was much the same in all of her life—she toiled, giving of herself so we would enjoy the fruit—a beautiful hand knit sweater, a warm piece of homemade bread. To be seated at her table and served a meal, prepared with such skill and love, was to feel a bit like royalty.

Her joy was in all of our happiness and comfort. How she loved her family. Yet, it extended beyond only family. Despite all the heartaches she experienced, she would always carry her head high and share her smile with all she met, often blessing them with a compliment or word of encouragement. "Think positively, darling!" she often prodded.

She forgot many things in her final years. She forgot how to roll her pie crust and although she tried until it was impossible, she forgot how to knit. To our horror, she forgot how to drive long before she was willing to give up her keys. But she never, to her very last days, lost her spirit and that smile that took us in and made us feel very important. It was the only thing she had left to give, and she did so freely.

For those who could not spend time with Gram these past years, be comforted to know her struggle is over—and it was a struggle. Fighter that she was, she did not intend to give up easily.

The prayer she prayed in our home, until she forgot even this, was that each one in her family, naming every one, "would live a long and happy life, going to church each week."

The example she left to me was found in her garden. Many times in the twenty-five years I knew her, I saw the weeds creep in and try to destroy its beauty. She would get down on her knees, pull out what she could, and plant something beautiful in all the barren spaces so they didn't stand a chance. This was how she lived her life.

I will always treasure her example and hope to see that smile again in his presence.

✝   ✝   ✝

When Jamie finished reading, Ed stood facing the family members and friends who had gathered. He thanked everyone for coming, then bowed his head to pray. As he raised his head and opened his Bible to read the passage he had selected, our eyes were drawn to a branch directly above his head.

"Oh, look!"

There on the bare branch sat the most stunning red bird with black wings—so vivid an image against the clear blue sky. All eyes were on him. My brother Jeff, standing beside my mother, extended an arm toward the bird, and as her eyes followed to catch a glimpse they looked over at me to share their delight.

"Scarlet Tanager!" we called out in unison as if meeting an old friend.

It was as if we had finally been reunited with that special moment in our past when we were privileged to care for that wild bird. It was so dependent on us for a while and then was gone.

We watched it for a moment—and then just as Flair had left us—it was gone.

Ed smiled as he watched it fly off, then opened his Bible.

"I'd like to read a portion of Psalm 90," he began.

Lord, you have been our dwelling place
throughout all generations.

Before the mountains were born
or you brought forth the earth and the world,
from everlasting to everlasting you are God.

You turn men back to dust,
saying, "Return to dust, O sons of men."
For a thousand years in your sight
are like a day that has just gone by,
or like a watch in the night.
You sweep men away in the sleep of death;
they are like the new grass of the morning—
though in the morning it springs up new,
by evening it is dry and withered.

We are consumed by your anger
and terrified by your indignation.
You have set our iniquities before you,
Our secret sins in the light of your presence.
All our days pass away under your wrath;
We finish our years with a moan.
The length of our days is seventy years—
or eighty, if we have the strength;
yet their span is but trouble and sorrow,
for they quickly pass, and we fly away. (NIV)

"We've come together to bury Gram," he continued, "to return her to the dust from which she came.

"Our lives are very complex, but I think I can outline Gram's life briefly. She had a troubled childhood, but she shared so little of it—and then not until her later years. She enjoyed a faithful marriage, and she was a happy mother to her children. She endured life's troubles and heartaches with grace.

"She suffered a devastating tragedy with the sudden loss of her beloved husband. Those of us who were close to her know that she almost did not recover from that loss. During this period she worked obsessively. She learned to paint, trying to put her life back together. But if the truth were told, I think she would have rather died along with him

"About twenty-five years ago, she found faith and enjoyed a renewed life. She attended church and read her Bible. Man, did she read her Bible. More than anyone I ever saw.

"And I almost forgot. She struggled through the long good-bye. She fought hard to ward off the ever-advancing, inevitably fatal effects of her disease. The stories we could tell you! The past year, for the most part, was a time of quiet and contentment for her.

"She was a real mother to me.

"We will miss her.

"And now, let us pray."

✠ ✠ ✠

I raised my head and looked beyond the grave. I hope I will never forget what I saw—my son Christopher, my handsome redhead, dressed as I hadn't seen him dressed in years. Far more important than his clothing was his smile. It was a radiant smile directed toward me, beaming with new life. My heart overflowed with praise to God for this wonderful answer to prayer.

This was not a sad day or a sad funeral, I thought. *It was a day of new beginnings.*

I thought of Gram, how like that lovely, independent bird, so dependent on us for awhile, and now truly free—free from her suffering, whole again in His presence.

And our son is truly home again.

"Christ bearer!"

The Lord is faithful.

We said our good-byes to friends and escorted Flip and her sister Liz to the car. They would travel home with Ed and me.

"Well, this is the close of a chapter in our life, hon," Ed said as we traveled home with a pensive, somewhat profound tone in his voice.

I breathed a sigh of great relief.

As we entered the Delaware Water Gap, I leaned my head back

heavily on the seat and looked up into the hills to perhaps snatch a memory of one of our wonderful adventures up there.

Reaching over, I rested my hand on top of Ed's as I often did, hoping to pass on a bit of the warmth and wonder that filled my mind. Yes, perhaps now there would be a time of peace and healing in the Walsh home. Ed glanced over as if we were thinking much the same thoughts.

As an eighteen-wheel tractor trailer lumbered by us, Flip broke the warm silence.

"My, Edward—the trucks are getting bigger every year!" she said in amazement, as if she had made a new discovery.

Ed removed his sunglasses—we looked at one another in disbelief.

We looked away from one another and up into the crags at the very top of the gap—where the golden eagle soars, and only an occasional rattlesnake disturbs the peace. A Psalm filled my heart:

> *I lift up my eyes to the hills—*
> *where does my help come from?*
> *My help comes from the Lord,*
> *the Maker of heaven and earth.*
> *He will not let your foot slip—*
> *he who watches over you will not slumber;*
> *indeed, he who watches over Israel*
> *will neither slumber nor sleep.*
> *The Lord watches over you—*
> *the Lord is your shade at your right hand;*
> *the sun will not harm you by day,*
> *nor the moon by night.*
> *The Lord will keep you from all harm—*
> *he will watch over your life;*
> *the Lord will watch over your coming and going*
> *both now and forevermore.*

PSALM 121, NIV

Amen!

I've often heard it said, "Growing old isn't for the cowardly."

Having been so intimately involved these past years with Gram and Flip, I developed an affinity toward the elderly. When I am held up behind an eighty-year-old man pushing a shopping cart alone through a store, I realize the tremendous efforts that have been exerted for him to be there at all. Most likely his vision is impaired considerably, and it would be safe to assume he is experiencing some sort of pain somewhere in his body. I see that there's something heroic in his even being at the store.

I have been privileged these past several years to be a part of some very memorable heroic last ventures. Each lasted only minutes, yet each one ended with a cheer.

One fall evening, just before dark, Ed and I were in the yard tossing the ball to David. Dawn joined us and before long we were pitching and batting balls. Flip was sitting on the sidelines in a chair next to Gram, observing.

"Hey, Flip! Come over here and hit the ball!" Ed yelled.

"Oh, Edward, I can't hit the ball!" she insisted.

"Oh, c'mon, try!"

Flip slowly stood up, walked over, and took the bat that was obviously awkward for her frail little frame.

Gram, now eighty-two and several years into her disease, sat fully dressed in a suit with stockings and heels, taking everything in as best she could.

"She can't hit that, Edward!" she kept saying.

Ed pitched the ball, and Flip swung hard. Blind in one eye with only partial vision in the other eye, she was not doing well.

"Oh, Margaretta, you can't hit that ball!" Gram insisted. It was beginning to sound like a challenge.

"Now, Gram, don't discourage Flip. Let's see *you* hit the ball!"

To our surprise she rose swiftly to her feet and walked over—high heels and all—and took the bat from Margaretta. Ed pitched the ball, not quite sure she would know what to do.

She hit it—not far, but she hit it.

He pitched the ball a second time. She hit it again, a bit farther. We were all amazed. It seemed she couldn't miss it. She looked quite serious. Ed stood back and pitched the ball a third time. This time she swung with a vengeance, clobbering the ball deep into the woods behind the yard. Bat in hand, she ran a complete circle around the yard and back to her batting position.

We all applauded and cheered, "Home run, Gram!"

(Oh, for a video camera!)

She gave Flip a look as if to say, "So there, Margaretta," and returned to her chair.

The second "heroic last venture" was priceless.

One morning as I sat waiting for Flip in a doctor's office, a large van pulled up to the door. It was apparently a transport for the elderly. The door of the van opened, and the driver gave a hand to an elderly gentleman as he stepped carefully to the ground. He appeared to be at least ninety, maybe older. He had a white, neatly trimmed beard, a top hat, a long, gray, tailored wool coat, dressy black shoes, and a dapper cane topped with a bright gold handle. He motioned for the attendant to remove her hand from his arm. He was not able to walk normally, but shuffled his feet as he walked. It took a considerable amount of time for him to make any noticeable progress. As I sat watching him inch his way toward the door, proud and determined, I could hear myself cheering inside, "You can do it!" I noticed others in the room watching with equal anticipation.

The driver held the door open as he continued to shuffle closer and closer toward the door. When he finally reached it, with great effort he lifted each foot individually, placing them inside the door. Finally inside, he stood tall, threw up his arms and, with a smile that lit up the room, announced: "I'm still alive!"

Everyone cheered.

✠   ✠   ✠

For this memorable moment I did have a video camera: My dad, seventy-five, had been hospitalized due to a fractured spine and complications with diabetes. It was touch-and-go as to whether he would make it. We were all greatly relieved and so thankful that he did pull through, but were all aware his condition was weakened. Having lost most of the vision in one eye, 50 percent in the other, and the use of one leg, a visit to our home was quite an undertaking.

He stepped outside the house and was noticeably intrigued with Jamie's new motorcycle. His mind was as sharp as ever; it just happened to be trapped in his frail body.

"Want to go for a ride, Grandpa?" Jamie asked.

Surely he was joking, I thought.

"Really?" my dad asked. "I'd love to!"

I couldn't believe my eyes. I tried to discourage the event, but as he put on the helmet and somehow got his bad leg over the seat behind Jamie, I ran into the house to grab the video camera. I prayed as I filmed. As they pulled out of the driveway and took off around the block, I could hear the roar of the 600cc racing engine as it steadily built up speed. It sounded like it was moving fast. I could only hope both wheels were on the ground! I continued to pray. They returned moments later up the driveway. My dad slowly hopped off and removed his helmet.

He let out a shrill—"O-O-O-E-E-E!

"I wouldn't have missed that for anything!" he added.

My mom apparently had no idea what had gone on during that

short time he had stepped outside the house. When I showed her the video months later, she was not nearly as excited as he had been.

I hesitate, though, to call this a "heroic last venture." You never know with my dad. After all, he's only seventy-five, and I know for a fact he's never tried rappelling, Australian style!

FROM THE JOURNAL OF MARY WALSH
April 1997

It is with a heavy heart that I reopen this chapter. I believed that it was complete—cute little ending, "rappelling, Australian style." However, my dad surprised us with the most heroic last venture of all.

My dad was hospitalized with kidney failure in February. Although we knew he was a very sick man we had good hope that he would improve with the dialysis treatments.

Only a few short weeks earlier, on January twenty-fifth, my family surprised my parents with a fiftieth anniversary party. My dad had not been feeling well the week before but was able to attend on that particular Saturday. It was, as my mom has described it, "as a dream." They restated their marriage vows and were united with friends and relatives they had not seen for many years. Within a day or two my dad was very ill, unable to eat. After a week at home he was admitted to the hospital ICU unit. Kidney failure was diagnosed.

Further testing revealed that his liver was also affected. His doctor assured us it would improve.

I would have to write another book altogether to adequately describe my dad, the unique individual that he has always been.

I loved the way friends described him:

"A man who never runs out of ideas."

"He has the ability to make everyone feel important and special."

"He fills a room."

"Talented? Incredible!"

While in the hospital he had a steady stream of visitors, all wishing for moments to share his wit and encouragement. During his pain-free moments he edited chapters of this book, encouraging me to complete it. Writing was but one of his many talents. He was a seasoned salesman and sold copies of his book How to Master the Radial Arm Saw *to several nurses. I seriously doubt any of them had ever set eyes on a radial arm saw.*

When further testing disclosed bone cancer, doctors believed it to be the very beginning stage. Dad hoped he would get better and get home but prepared for the worst. He spent his nights praying that he would be ready should the Lord take him. He had drawn close to the Lord during his final months and found real peace. He wanted to share it with his suffering roommates as they came and went. He knew they needed to find peace with God too.

✠   ✠   ✠

My Dad's great love was woodworking, and he was known throughout the woodworking world as Mr. Sawdust. Dad built many museum-quality reproductions of eighteenth-century furniture in his lifetime: grandfather clocks, highboys, cupboards, desks, and tables. He believed them to be better than a tombstone. When he could no longer see well enough to do or teach woodworking, he retired to his computer, where he spent many years writing. He completed a compelling novel about his boyhood memories, *A Missouri Incident,* and worked on the completion of a work, *The Kunkel Family in America.* It was started by his mother and was probably the most complete family genealogy of its kind. His latest project, which Ed planned to help him accomplish, he called "GEN 2000." His hope was to see the year 2000 and to have his completed genealogy up on the Internet, so it could be freely accessed for years to come.

His doctors sent him home, hoping he might improve. My dad knew that time was of the essence. So did Ed. My brothers no sooner got him into the house than this heroic last venture began to quickly take shape.

"Mom, you don't really want this couch in here, do you?" my brother Carl asked, lifting one end as Wally lifted the other. Just as quickly, Dad's computer desk was moved into the living room in its place.

"What's going on?" Mom asked. The entire living room was rearranged.

Ed and I drove from Pennsylvania, unloaded Ed's fastest computer and walked into the house. There stood my dad, frail, but thrilled with all the commotion.

He hugged Ed and cried, "You've been just like a son to me. I love you, Ed." It was true. Dad was Ed's first boss. He was also his biggest booster since the start of his business. He shared the excitement through the years of all his successes and truly shared in the frustration of the lawsuit. It was as if it were his business as well.

In recent years, Ed had spent countless hours with him in his office helping him on his computer to accomplish the many things he wanted to do. Together they created my dad's own Web page for the sale of his latest woodworking book. They really kept one another creating and dreaming. "Sometimes I think I'm keeping his heart going!" Ed said recently.

They were good for each other.

"I love you too, Dad. We've got work to do!"

Dad stood gazing at the completed arrangement: the computer on top of the sprawling white Formica desk surrounded by his stately grandfather clock and a few of his favorite pieces of furniture.

"It's beautiful! It looks almost ethereal!" he said.

As Ed sat at the computer, Dad sat in a chair watching as pages of his genealogy began to appear on the screen—old photographs, etchings, literally hundreds of pages of work—representing fifty years of research. He gave instructions and suggestions, stopping when he got tired.

Their mission was accomplished. The Kunkel family would have its place in cyberspace!

That night Dad was rushed back to the hospital by ambulance, where his condition continued to deteriorate. He died a few weeks later on April sixth.

We suffered a tremendous loss as a family. I was amazed how many people told me, "I lost my best friend!" Yet I am thankful for the fact that he had truly made his peace with God.

I look at the pieces of furniture in my home that he made so skillfully, so lovingly. Each one has mellowed and become richer with time, just as he always said they would. They bring to mind this man I loved so dearly, and you know, he was right—they are better than a tombstone.

$\mathscr{I}$ treasure the ability of the mind to record memories in such incredible detail. Not only the sights and sounds of a moment in time, but the smells, sensations, and emotions. It is truly amazing! To be able to recall at will a particular time or event in my past is a blessing I no longer take for granted.

One icy winter's night as I sat pondering Christmas, I recaptured a glimpse of Christmas Eve the year I was five years old. Looking out the window into the still night, more and more of a very special memory took shape in my mind. The more I thought about it the more I wanted to share it, so I sat down and wrote what I recalled. I sent it along with my Christmas cards to a few friends and relatives. The memory was as follows:

CHRISTMAS EVE 1956
O come all ye faithful.
Joyful and triumphant,
O come ye, o come ye to Bethlehem. . . .

My eyes were drawn to seven stockings hung beneath the mantle. I quickly matched each glittered name with a brother singing his very loudest, carols reserved especially for this night. As we encircled the piano, Dad played with purpose. "This is the real meaning of Christmas," each resounding chord reminded us. Tomorrow at the first glimmer of dawn we would find each stocking overflowing—just as my young heart felt at this moment. My brothers, Dad and Mom, Christmas Eve—what more could a five-year-old girl want?

I glanced out the window into the night so still. Snow was falling silently, draping our familiar world in soft flannel. It would be a white Christmas for sure.

A muffled voice broke through the darkness, as a stranger lost in the storm, desperate for someone to hear. Faintly it came. The playing stopped as we stood motionless, hoping to hear it once again.

"It's a boy! We have a boy!"

Dad threw open the window and a gust of chilly winter air swept in the joyous news. Little Nanny Lucy leaned out our neighbor's window, waving her arms ecstatically, heralding the birth of her great-grandson, Jimmy John. He would be a welcome addition to the family of three daughters.

Waiting hot chocolate topped off the excitement before heading up to bed.

As I lay awake, gazing out at the full winter moon, I pondered the words we had sung.

Joy to the world,
The Lord is come,
Let earth receive her King.

An only son had been born tonight, bringing joy which could not be contained. They wanted to share it with the world—kind of like the angels so long ago. God's only Son, born on a night such as this—yet, more than just a babe he was . . .

Wonderful Counselor
Mighty God
Everlasting Father
Prince of Peace

I thought back a year, remembering my oldest brother, Marc, pointing out the silhouette of Santa's reindeer crossing in front of the moon outside my window. I was sure I saw it too.

How could I sleep?

But this year was different. I closed my eyes and slept so peacefully—I was not looking for reindeer, for I had heard the angels sing.

This is obviously a happy memory to me. Happy memories as well as painful, unpleasant ones are all a part of me. There is security in remembering my loving dad and mom, my brothers, our home, the excitement at the sight of snow, the birth of Jesus.

I remember falling in love with my husband, the joyous day I became his wife, the birth of each of our children, the loss of our twins. They all bring me to where I am now.

I have enjoyed writing this book. I believe that apart from the treasure I have laid up in heaven, memories are my greatest possessions. To have these pictures—so much a part of me—taken away little by little would be so terrifying.

To gradually lose everything one precious memory at a time is precisely the course that this disease takes.

"There's a day coming when I won't remember my own name!" Gram would say very early in the disease. She realized she was becoming forgetful. But it went far beyond that.

This most ruthless, relentless disease does not give up until it has taken it all. Gram displayed insecurity and was often in near terror. She could not rest. She would make trip after trip, up and down the stairs, trying to hold on as it all slipped away.

I believe, though, that her greatest suffering occurred during the early stage of the disease, soon after we moved. She was keenly aware that she was becoming extremely forgetful. It was very distressing to her. When she was no longer capable of driving, she became severely depressed. One day, she pleaded with Ed to "give her some pills" so that she might die. And that was only the beginning.

Her agitated behavior became so incredibly bizarre that it wore the family down. For extended periods of time there was no letup—day or night—and few answers to be found anywhere. It was so very hard. There are medications that provide some relief for agitated behavior in some Alzheimer's patients. But in Gram's case, medication merely took the edge off. It was a constant, seemingly futile effort to control and reassure her.

When the family is emotionally drained, the caregiving demands shift and become physically demanding. There are round-the-clock activities such as bathing, changing, and feeding. When the time comes to consider a nursing home, we found out that is easier said than done.

Years ago, we naively promised Gram that we would never put her in a nursing home. That promise continued to hang heavily over our heads. It's a promise I would advise others not to make. Promise instead to do whatever is best for everyone involved.

As the disease progressed, there were definite moments of reckoning. We took special note of the events that made it clear something was very wrong. They were subtle at first, such as her brakeless drive down Schooley's Mountain Road and the minor surgery she performed on her nose. But then an event would jolt us. Such was the case when she no longer recognized her sister and lifelong companion. To see her look squarely into her sister's eyes and ask, "Where is Margaretta?" was alarming. Then to watch her spend the next six months looking for her, night and day, was heartbreaking.

Finding her wedding ring on the ground was another sad moment. There were so many, and with each came the realization that she was slipping away—and we mourned.

There is a truth about this disease that needs to be understood. By the time we actually said good-bye to Gram, we for the most part had mourned her loss. Family members and friends who are not around to see the regression need to understand this. There is an ongoing grieving process and moral support, phone calls, and visits are vital throughout the process.

It is so unlike any other disease in which the body, not the mind, fails.

To those who are aware of someone caring for a person with Alzheimer's, possibly a family member, someone in your church, there are very practical ways to help.

Make a phone call. Ask questions. Don't assume everything is under control. It may not be. Offer to make a trip to the store or sit for a few hours to relieve the family. This kind of encouragement means so much.

A dear friend, Nancy, came many Saturdays during Gram's last year to help bathe her and clean their apartment. She was such an encouragement to Flip and I. Gram would smile as if meeting her for the first time. She could always sense when someone was there because he or she wanted to be.

If Gram did not want to get in the tub or go into another room, she would grab on to a door molding leaving no way to move her. If she did not want to sit down in the tub, there was simply no way to get her to do it. She remained physically strong until her last days although she weighed only ninety-five pounds at the end.

Getting her to bed at night was always a challenge. Flip would attempt to coax her out of her chair.

"No!" She would not get up.

I would attempt to lift her from the chair. We would try and try—often getting quite frustrated. We would call Jamie. He had found a way to get her into the room almost every time.

My tall, handsome son would graciously walk over to her chair. She would look up at him and smile as if she had seen Prince Charming. Jamie would extend his hand.

"Would you care to dance?" he would ask her. She would stand up, delighted, and holding him close, they would dance toward the bedroom door. On occasion she would see where all this was leading to, grab on to the door and put up a fight. Then we'd have to resort to Edward. She would always listen to him.

This experience brought out the best and the worst in each of us. I thought I was a patient person, yet there were moments of testing that I failed miserably. One icy morning in late December stands out particularly in my mind. Gram had developed one of the deepest, nagging coughs I had ever heard. Had it gone into pneumonia? We headed for her doctor to find out.

She was going to make her appearance in her silky, short-sleeved blouse—and that was it. She would have it no other way. She refused to put on a coat or a jacket or a sweater. Often I could overlook insignificant details to avoid conflict, but this was not one of those times. She did end up wearing a jacket, and we were unfashionably late, but I was no longer included among her favorite people.

Watching my husband care for his grandmother so tenderly through the years has made his promise to "always love me, no matter what" very believable.

We were not a part of a nearby church. We had only a few friends in the area, but they were most supportive. As in so many of life's trials, our desire was for this one to be lifted out of our hands altogether. I desired that many times throughout those years. But that is not usually God's way.

Although the Lord is able to do just that, more often we must go through the trials all the way, holding on to the promise that he will be with us.

WHEN YOU PASS THROUGH THE WATERS, I WILL BE WITH YOU; AND WHEN YOU PASS THROUGH THE RIVERS, THEY WILL NOT SWEEP OVER YOU. WHEN YOU WALK THROUGH THE FIRE, YOU WILL NOT BE BURNED; THE FLAMES WILL NOT SET YOU ABLAZE.   ISAIAH 43:2, NIV

God's way:

HE COMFORTS US IN ALL OUR TROUBLES SO THAT WE CAN COMFORT OTHERS. WHEN OTHERS ARE TROUBLED, WE WILL BE ABLE TO GIVE THEM THE SAME COMFORT GOD HAS GIVEN US.   2 CORINTHIANS 1:4, NLT

We are to:

SHARE EACH OTHER'S TROUBLES AND PROBLEMS, AND IN THIS WAY OBEY THE LAW OF CHRIST.   GALATIANS 6:2, NLT

The greatest challenge throughout the past seven years was keeping my eyes on the Lord and his promise to never forsake me.

Though I failed miserably in this area at times, another beautiful psalm of David reassured me time and again:

> AS A FATHER HAS COMPASSION ON HIS CHILDREN, SO THE LORD HAS COMPASSION ON THOSE WHO FEAR HIM; FOR HE KNOWS HOW WE ARE FORMED, HE REMEMBERS THAT WE ARE DUST. PSALM 103:13-14, NIV

✛　✛　✛

Following an extended, much-needed period of rest, Flip is doing well. It does not appear that there will be a sequel after all.

✛　✛　✛

Throughout the troubled years we experienced with Christopher, we had the faithful support of a couple who lived nearby. I don't know what we would have done without them!

The last portion of Proverbs 18:24 speaks of "a friend who sticks closer than a brother" (NIV).

Not only were they a constant source of support and encouragement to Ed and I, but I believe they were very instrumental in reaching Chris. They took the time to reach out to him, talk to him, even arranged a meeting in our home. Mannie and Sharon, I thank you both from the bottom of my heart.

✛　✛　✛

I hope in some small way my story will lighten your load, even if you can just see that God is faithful. He will see you through!

And you will praise him in the end.

From the journal of Mary Walsh

Maybe that is where I got the idea.

At the end of the fairy tale, filled with wicked stepsisters, backbreaking work, and rejection, Cinderella rides off into the sunset with her Prince Charming. What child wouldn't sigh contentedly and drop off to a pleasant sleep?

It is New Year's Day, the first day of a new year—a new millennium. The year begins as it has for sixteen years, with the anniversary of the birth and death of our twins. This event begins each year with mixed emotions, hope, and humble trust for the unknown providence ahead. As I look over the events of the past year, I realize that I cannot end it with that welcome and longed for conclusion, "and they all lived happily ever after!"

That ending is reserved for fairy tales, I have come to see.

We were released from the lawsuit in August following a settlement between the two other parties.

Hurrah!

After three years of hardship and hassle and incalculable expense to the business, it was a day of bittersweet rejoicing—like walking out of prison after having served a sentence you did not deserve. Most costly of all was the obvious toll it had taken on Ed.

Where did I get the idea that happily ever after would begin with our wonderful conversion to Christ? Certainly I had found my Prince Charming. Maybe it was from that little tract that said that God loves you and has a wonderful plan for your life! Just as that Alzheimer's pamphlet needed some "fill in" information gained from experience, I see now that this statement, though also true, would have the details filled in as time went on.

Yes, it is a wonderful plan, but it is God's plan and not our own; surely his ways are not our ways. If they were mine, I would have twin sons, sixteen years old—and who knows the stories I could have told about them!

But God's plan was to take them to heaven and teach me one of the most profound lessons of my life—he is in control and can comfort us in the deepest and darkest valleys of our lives.

Christopher's conversion—so wonderful!

And he lived happily ever after.

That would certainly be my ending of choice.

Forgiveness is a marvelous thing. The Psalm comes to mind:

FOR AS HIGH AS THE HEAVENS ARE ABOVE THE EARTH,
SO GREAT IS HIS LOVE FOR THOSE WHO FEAR HIM;
AS FAR AS THE EAST IS FROM THE WEST,
SO FAR HAS HE REMOVED OUR TRANSGRESSIONS FROM US.

PSALM 103:11-12, NIV

I have observed from others and my own life that there are consequences and scars from the sins of our past. The lost years and the nature of the sins in the path Chris took have made his progress difficult. But the story is not over, and the Bible's promise for him is true for any follower of Christ.

I AM SURE THAT GOD, WHO BEGAN THE GOOD WORK WITHIN YOU,
WILL CONTINUE HIS WORK UNTIL IT IS FINALLY FINISHED ON THAT
DAY WHEN CHRIST JESUS COMES BACK AGAIN. PHILIPPIANS 1:6, NLT

*But what about living happily ever after? I would like that
ending!*

*And it will be the ending. But it's reserved for after the battle
is fought and the race is won. For it is a battle, fierce and raging,
not without casualties. And it is a race to the finish—not on a
smooth track, but one resembling that path up the Appalachian
trail strewn with rocks and gnarled tree roots.*

*When it is over, and all tears have been wiped away, that
fairy-tale ending will at last come true.*

And they all lived happily ever after!

(There! I did it!)

☩   ☩   ☩

POP GOES THE WEASEL
It was the tune that made them giggle
    as she bounced them on her knee,
    When they were young and she so filled with joy.
    A tune that later filled our world from dusk 'til early dawn
    Still sung with all the gusto she'd employ.
Yet soon became the stanza
    and the tune that made heads turn
    Sung loudly through the aisles for all to hear,
    Just as a child, restraint now gone,
    I sometimes hoped that tune would disappear—

Yet when it did, though peace restored,
*   After oh, so very long,*
*   I realized we had said good-bye—*
*   to more than just a song.*
M. Walsh